REPENTANCE

REPENTANCE

PRESIDENT EZRA TAFT BENSON
ELDER MARVIN J. ASHTON
ELDER NEAL A. MAXWELL
ELDER M. RUSSELL BALLARD
ELDER RICHARD G. SCOTT
ELDER MARION D. HANKS
ELDER J. RICHARD CLARKE
ELDER LOREN C. DUNN
ELDER VAUGHN J. FEATHERSTONE
ELDER HUGH W. PINNOCK
ELDER RONALD E. POELMAN
ELDER F. BURTON HOWARD
BISHOP ROBERT D. HALES
ELDER THEODORE M. BURTON

Deseret Book Company
Salt Lake City, Utah

©1990 Deseret Book Company

Library of Congress Cataloging-in-Publication Data

Repentance / by Ezra Taft Benson . . . [et al.].
   p. cm.
   Includes bibliographical references and index.
   ISBN 0-87579-424-6
   1. Spiritual life—Mormon authors. 2. Repentance—Mormon Church.
3. Church of Jesus Christ of Latter-day Saints—Doctrines.
4. Mormon Church—Doctrines. I. Benson, Ezra Taft.
BX8656.R43 1990
248.4'8933—dc20   90-43965
                                          CIP

Printed in the United States of America
10   9   8   7   6   5   4   3   2   1

CONTENTS

A MIGHTY CHANGE OF HEART 1
PRESIDENT EZRA TAFT BENSON

THE MEANING OF REPENTANCE... 9
ELDER THEODORE M. BURTON

GOD'S PLAN OF HAPPINESS 23
ELDER NEAL A. MAXWELL

THE REWARDS OF REPENTANCE... 36
ELDER F. BURTON HOWARD

BEGINNING AGAIN 44
ELDER HUGH W. PINNOCK

GOD'S LOVE FOR US TRANSCENDS
OUR TRANSGRESSIONS 51
ELDER RONALD E. POELMAN

"FORGIVE THEM, I PRAY THEE".... 57
ELDER VAUGHN J. FEATHERSTONE

THE LORD OFFERS EVERYONE
A WAY BACK..................... 66
BISHOP ROBERT D. HALES

CONTENTS

LET MERCY TEMPER JUSTICE 72
ELDER THEODORE M. BURTON

HE MEANS ME 79
ELDER MARION D. HANKS

TIME IS ON YOUR SIDE............ 86
ELDER LOREN C. DUNN

CONFESSION: A REQUIREMENT
FOR FORGIVENESS................ 91
ELDER J. RICHARD CLARKE

BEGIN NOW TO KEEP
THE COMMANDMENTS 95
ELDER M. RUSSELL BALLARD

WE LOVE YOU—
PLEASE COME BACK..............104
ELDER RICHARD G. SCOTT

WHILE THEY ARE WAITING........110
ELDER MARVIN J. ASHTON

INDEX 119

A MIGHTY CHANGE OF HEART

PRESIDENT EZRA TAFT BENSON

In the usual sense of the term, *Church membership* means that a person has his or her name officially recorded on the membership records of the Church. By that definition, we have more than six million members of the Church.

But the Lord defines a member of His kingdom in quite a different way. In 1828, through the Prophet Joseph Smith, He said, "Behold, this is my doctrine—whosoever repenteth and cometh unto me, *the same is my church*." (D&C 10:67; italics added.) To Him whose church this is, membership involves far more than simply being a member of record.

I would therefore like to set forth important concepts that we must understand and apply if we are to truly repent and come unto the Lord.

One of Satan's most frequently used deceptions is the notion that the commandments of God are meant to restrict freedom and limit happiness. Young people especially sometimes feel that the standards of the Lord are like fences and chains, blocking them from those activities that seem most enjoyable in life.

But exactly the opposite is true. The gospel plan is *the*

1

plan by which men are brought to a fulness of joy. This is the first concept I wish to stress: The gospel principles are the steps and guidelines that will help us find true happiness and joy. The understanding of this concept caused the Psalmist to exclaim, "O how I love thy law! . . . Thou through thy commandments hast made me wiser than mine enemies. . . . Thy word is a lamp unto my feet, and a light unto my path. . . . Thy testimonies have I taken as an heritage forever: for they are the rejoicing of my heart." (Ps. 119:97–98, 105, 111.)

If we wish to truly repent and come unto Him so that we can be called members of His Church, we must first and foremost come to realize this eternal truth — the gospel plan is *the* plan of happiness. *Wickedness never did, never does, never will* bring us happiness. Violation of the laws of God brings only misery, bondage, and darkness.

A second concept that is important to our understanding is the relationship of repentance to the principle of faith. Repentance is the second fundamental principle of the gospel. The first is that we must have faith in the Lord Jesus Christ. Why is this so? Why must faith in the Lord precede true repentance?

To answer this question, we must understand something about the atoning sacrifice of the Master. Lehi taught that "no flesh . . . can dwell in the presence of God, save it be through the merits, and mercy, and grace of the Holy Messiah." (2 Ne. 2:8.) Even the most just and upright man cannot save himself solely on his own merits, for, as the Apostle Paul tells us, "All have sinned, and come short of the glory of God." (Rom. 3:23.) If it were not for the perfect, sinless life of the Savior, which He willingly laid down for us, there could be no remission of sins.

2

Therefore, repentance means more than simply a reformation of behavior. Many men and women in the world demonstrate great willpower and self-discipline in overcoming bad habits and the weaknesses of the flesh. Yet at the same time they give no thought to the Master, sometimes even openly rejecting Him. Such changes of behavior, even if in a positive direction, do not constitute repentance. Faith in the Lord Jesus Christ is the foundation upon which sincere and meaningful repentance must be built. If we truly seek to put away sin, we must first look to Him who is the Author of our salvation.

The third important principle for us to understand, if we would be true members of the Church, is that repentance involves not just a change of actions, but also a change of heart. When King Benjamin finished his remarkable address in the land of Zarahemla, the people all cried with one voice that they believed his words. They knew of a surety that his promises of redemption were true, because, said they, "The Spirit of the Lord Omnipotent . . . has wrought a mighty change in us, or in our hearts, [and note this] that we have no more disposition to do evil, but to do good continually." (Mosiah 5:2.)

When we have undergone this mighty change, which is brought about only through faith in Jesus Christ and through the operation of the Spirit upon us, it is as though we have become a new person. Thus, the change is likened to a new birth. Thousands of you have experienced this change. You have forsaken lives of sin, sometimes deep and offensive sin, and through applying the blood of Christ in your lives, have become clean. You have no more disposition to return to your old ways. You are in reality a new person. This is what is meant by a change of heart.

The fourth concept I would like to stress is what the scriptures term "godly sorrow" for our sins. It is not uncommon to find men and women in the world who feel remorse for the things they do wrong. Sometimes this is because their actions cause them or loved ones great sorrow and misery. Sometimes their sorrow is caused because they are caught and punished for their actions. Such worldly feelings do not constitute "godly sorrow."

Godly sorrow is vividly portrayed in two places in scripture. In the final days of the Nephite nation, Mormon said of his people: "Their sorrowing was not unto repentance, because of the goodness of God; but it was rather the sorrowing of the damned, because the Lord would not always suffer them to take happiness in sin. And they did not come unto Jesus with broken hearts and contrite spirits, but they did curse God, and wish to die." (Morm. 2:13–14.)

In the Eastern Hemisphere, the Apostle Paul labored among the people of Corinth. After reports came of serious problems among the Saints, including immorality (see 1 Cor. 5:1), Paul wrote a sharp letter of rebuke. The people responded in the proper spirit, and evidently the problems were corrected, for in his second epistle to them, Paul wrote: "Now I rejoice, not that ye were made sorry, but that ye sorrowed to repentance: for ye were made sorry after a godly manner. . . . For godly sorrow worketh repentance to salvation not to be repented of: but the sorrow of the world worketh death." (2 Cor. 7:9–10.)

In both of these scriptures, godly sorrow is defined as a sorrow that leads us to repentance. Godly sorrow is a gift of the Spirit. It is a deep realization that our actions have offended our Father and our God. It is the sharp and

4

keen awareness that our behavior caused the Savior, Him who knew no sin, even the greatest of all, to endure agony and suffering. Our sins caused Him to bleed at every pore. This very real mental and spiritual anguish is what the scriptures refer to as having "a broken heart and a contrite spirit." (3 Ne. 9:20; see also Moro. 6:2; D&C 20:37; 59:8; Ps. 34:18; 51:17; Isa. 57:15.) Such a spirit is the absolute prerequisite for true repentance.

The next principle I would like to discuss is this: No one is more anxious to see us change our lives than the Father and the Savior. In the book of Revelation is a powerful and profound invitation from the Savior. He says, "I stand at the door, and knock: if any man hear my voice, and open the door, I will come in to him." (Rev. 3:20.) Note that He does not say, "I stand at the door and wait for you to knock." He is calling, beckoning, asking that we simply open our hearts and let Him in.

In Moroni's great sermon on faith, the principle is even more clearly taught. He was told by the Lord, "If men come unto me I will show unto them their weakness. I give unto men weakness that they may be humble; and my grace is sufficient for all men." It matters not what is our lack or our weakness or our insufficiency. His gifts and powers are sufficient to overcome them all.

Moroni continues with the words of the Lord: "My grace is sufficient for all men that humble themselves before me; for if they humble themselves before me, and have faith in me, *then will I make weak things become strong unto them.*" (Ether 12:27; italics added.) What a promise from the Lord! The very source of our troubles can be changed, molded, and formed into a strength and a source of power.

This promise is repeated in one form or another in many other scriptures. Isaiah said, "He giveth power to the faint; and to them that have no might he increaseth strength." (Isa. 40:29.) Paul was told by the Lord, "My grace is sufficient for thee: for my strength is made perfect in weakness." (2 Cor. 12:9.) In the Doctrine and Covenants we read, "He that trembleth under my power shall be made strong, and shall bring forth fruits of praise and wisdom." (D&C 52:17; see also 1 Ne. 17:3; 2 Ne. 3:13; D&C 1:28; 133:58–59.)

We must take our sins to the Lord in humble and sorrowful repentance. We must plead with Him for power to overcome them. The promises are sure. He will come to our aid. We will find the power to change our lives.

The sixth and final point I wish to make about the process of repentance is that we must be careful, as we seek to become more and more godlike, that we do not become discouraged and lose hope. Becoming Christlike is a lifetime pursuit and very often involves growth and change that is slow, almost imperceptible. The scriptures record remarkable accounts of men whose lives changed dramatically, in an instant, as it were: Alma the Younger, Paul on the road to Damascus, Enos praying far into the night, King Lamoni. Such astonishing examples of the power to change even those steeped in sin give confidence that the Atonement can reach even those deepest in despair.

But we must be cautious as we discuss these remarkable examples. Though they are real and powerful, they are the exception more than the rule. For every Paul, for every Enos, and for every King Lamoni, there are hundreds and thousands of people who find the process of repentance much more subtle, much more imperceptible. Day by day they move closer to the Lord, little realizing they are building a godlike life. They live quiet lives of goodness, service, and commitment. They are like the Lamanites, who the Lord said "were baptized with fire and with the Holy Ghost, *and they knew it not.*" (3 Ne. 9:20; italics added.)

We must not lose hope. Hope is an anchor to the souls of men. Satan would have us cast away that anchor. In this way he can bring discouragement and surrender. But we must not lose hope. The Lord is pleased with every effort, even the tiny, daily ones in which we strive to be more like Him. Though we may see that we have far to go on the road to perfection, we must not give up hope.

So, as we seek to qualify to be members of Christ's church—members in the sense in which He uses the term, members who have repented and come unto Him—let us remember these six principles. First, the gospel is the Lord's plan of happiness, and repentance is designed to bring us joy. Second, true repentance is based on and flows from faith in the Lord Jesus Christ. There is no other way. Third, true repentance involves a change of heart and not just a change of behavior. Fourth, part of this mighty change of heart is to feel godly sorrow for our sins. This is what is meant by a broken heart and a contrite spirit. Fifth, God's gifts are sufficient to help us overcome every sin and weakness if we will but turn to Him for help. Finally, we must remember that most repentance does not involve sensational or dramatic changes, but rather is a step-by-step, steady, and consistent movement toward godliness.

If we will strive to incorporate these principles into our lives and implement them on a daily basis, we shall then

7

qualify to be more than members of record in the church of Jesus Christ. As true members, we have claim to His promise: "Whosoever is of my church, and endureth of my church to the end, him will I establish upon my rock, and the gates of hell shall not prevail against them." (D&C 10:69.) May we all win that promise for ourselves.

THE MEANING OF REPENTANCE

ELDER THEODORE M. BURTON

All of us need to understand and appreciate that repentance is the mechanism for personal growth and development. Repentance is so fundamental that the Lord gave a revelation to Oliver Cowdery through the Prophet Joseph Smith in which he said: "Say nothing but repentance unto this generation: keep my commandments, and assist to bring forth my work, according to my commandments, and you shall be blessed." (D&C 6:9.)

The Lord repeated this statement word for word to Hyrum Smith as recorded in Doctrine & Covenants 11:9. Later he gave two other identical revelations on repentance, one to John Whitmer, the other to Peter Whitmer, with one revelation following the other, concluding with these words: "And now, behold, I say unto you, that the thing which will be of the most worth unto you will be to *declare repentance unto this people,* that you may bring souls unto me, that you may rest with them in the kingdom of my Father." (D&C 15:6; 16:6; italics added.)

Why would the Lord give two identical revelations — and have them published in the Doctrine and Covenants — one following the other word for word, unless they were

9

especially intended to be given not only to the Whitmers, but also to all of us?

Actually, I must repent for saying that the two revelations are identical—there *is* one word that is different, but very important. In section 15, the fourth word is "John," and in section 16, the fourth word is "Peter." I feel justified in applying these revelations to all of us because of this repeated instruction. In the first revelation, I can place my own name so that it is addressed to me: "Hearken, my servant Theodore!" In the second revelation, you can insert your own name to make it apply to you: "Hearken, my servant Bill," or "my handmaiden Sue"! Thus these revelations can apply to you and to me to help us understand that the thing of greatest worth to each of us is to declare repentance, not only to others, but to ourselves as well. In fact, the importance of repentance is stressed seventy-one times in the Doctrine and Covenants alone! The Lord is a master teacher and knows the value of repetition in learning. It is time to understand why and how repentance is a matter of such great worth to you in your individual life!

THE MEANING OF REPENTANCE

Just what *is* repentance? Actually it is easier for me to tell you what repentance is *not* than to tell you what repentance *is*.

One of my assignments as a General Authority was to assist the First Presidency in preparing information for them to use in considering applications to readmit transgressors into the Church and to restore priesthood and/or temple blessings. Many times a bishop will write: "I feel he has suffered enough!" But suffering is not repentance.

10

Suffering comes from *lack* of complete repentance. A stake president will write: "I feel he has been punished enough!" But punishment is not repentance. Punishment *follows* disobedience and *precedes* repentance. A husband will write: "My wife has confessed everything!" But confession is not repentance. Confession is an admission of guilt that occurs *as* repentance begins. A wife will write: "My husband is filled with remorse!" But remorse is not repentance. Remorse and sorrow continue because a person has *not* yet fully repented. But if suffering, punishment, confession, remorse, and sorrow are not repentance, what *is* repentance?

REPENTANCE IN THE OLD TESTAMENT

To answer this question, let us go back to the Old Testament. The Old Testament was written in Hebrew, and the word used for this concept of repentance is *shube*. Let me read a passage from Ezekiel 33:8–11 and insert the word *shube* into the English translation to help us understand what repentance is: "When I say unto the wicked, O wicked man, thou shalt surely die; if thou dost not speak to warn the wicked from his way, that wicked man shall die in his iniquity; but his blood will I require at thine hand. Nevertheless, if thou warn the wicked of his way to [*shube,* or] turn from his way and live: [*shube, shube!*] turn ye, turn ye from your evil ways: for why will ye die, O house of Israel?"

I know of no kinder, sweeter passage in the Old Testament than those beautiful lines. Can you hear a kind, wise, gentle, loving Father in Heaven pleading with you to *shube* or turn back to him, to leave unhappiness, sorrow, regret, and despair behind and now turn back to your

Father's family where you can find happiness, joy, and acceptance among his other children? In the Father's family, you are surrounded with love and affection. That is the message of the Old Testament, and prophet after prophet writes of *shube,* which is that turning back to the family of the Lord where you can be received with joy and rejoicing. There is an implicit message there that we in the family of Jesus Christ ought never forget. We must receive the former transgressor back into this family with open arms and comfort and bless him for making the change.

That is what Isaiah had in mind when he wrote: "Seek ye the Lord while he may be found, call ye upon him while he is near; let the wicked forsake his way, and the unrighteous man his thoughts: and let him [*shube,* or] return unto the Lord, and he will have mercy upon him; and to our God, for he will abundantly pardon [if he will only *shube*]." (Isa. 55:6–7.)

Throughout the Old Testament, a fundamental theme is forsaking or turning from evil and doing instead that which is noble and good. Not only must we change our ways; we must as well change our very thoughts, which control our actions. Repentance is turning back to God!

REPENTANCE IN THE NEW TESTAMENT

Let us now turn to the New Testament, which was written in Greek. How did those Greek writers translate the word *shube* into Greek and still retain its concept of repentance? They used the word *metaneoeo,* which is a compound word of two parts. The first part, *meta,* we use as a prefix in our English vocabulary. When we eat, we convert food by a process of metabolism into fat, muscle, and connective tissue. When we see a crawling caterpillar

12

stop, attach itself to a limb, and spin a cocoon, the insect inside its silken case undergoes metamorphosis. It changes its form into a moth or a beautiful butterfly. The prefix *meta,* then, refers to change.

The second part of the word *metaneoeo* is subject to various spellings. The letter *n,* for instance, is sometimes transliterated as *pn,* as in the French word *pneu,* meaning an air-filled tire. We also find *pneu* in our word pneumatic, as, for instance, a pneumatic hammer or a pneumatic drill, which are air-driven tools. It is also found in our word pneumonia, which is an air sickness of the lungs. There are several spellings of this root and many meanings attached to this word, like air, mind, thought, thinking, or spirit, depending on how it is used.

The Greek usage of words is similar to that of English, as, for example, with the word *spirit.* To a child, spirit might mean a ghost; to you, spirit may mean influence, such as team spirit or the spirit of Elijah. But to me — since I was an organic chemist during my university years — or to a pharmacist, spirit simply means ethyl alcohol. In the context where *meta* and *neoeo* are used in the New Testament, the word *metaneoeo* means a change of mind or thought or thinking so powerful and so strong that it changes our very way of life. I think *metaneoeo* is an excellent translation of *shube.* The meaning of both these words is to turn or change from evil to righteousness and to God.

But trouble came when Greek was translated into Latin. Only the educated people spoke Greek. When the New Testament was translated into Latin for the use of the common people who spoke that language, an unfortunate choice was made in translation. *Metaneoeo* was translated

13

into the word *poenitere*. The root *poen* in that word is the same root found in our English words punish, penance, penitent, and repentance. So the beautiful meaning of Hebrew and Greek was changed in Latin to an ugly meaning involving hurting, punishing, whipping, cutting, mutilating, disfiguring, starving, or even torturing. Small wonder then that most people have come to fear and dread the word repentance, which they were taught and now understand to mean repeated or never-ending punishment. People must somehow be made to realize that the true meaning of repentance is that we do not require people to be punished or to punish themselves, but to change their lives so they can escape eternal punishment. If they have this understanding, it will relieve their anxiety and fears and become a welcome and treasured word in our religious vocabulary.

THREE STEPS OF REPENTANCE

Let me read again to you from Ezekiel 33, which outlines three main steps of repentance: (1) commitment, (2) restitution, and (3) forsaking sin. "If the wicked restore the pledge, give again that he had robbed, walk in the statutes of life, without committing iniquity: he shall surely live, he shall not die." (V. 15.)

"RESTORE THE PLEDGE"

Let us analyze these three steps of repentance. The first thing to do is to "restore the pledge," and this is the most difficult step in the repentance process. But what does the statement "restore the pledge" mean?

To restore the pledge means to renew one's covenant with the Lord. Forget all excuses and finally recognize fully, exactly, what you have done. Don't say, "If I hadn't been so angry," "If my parents had only been more strict," "If my bishop had only been more understanding," "If my teachers had only taught me better," "If it hadn't been so dark," "If I hadn't been so hungry," "If the stake president had only helped me to understand," etc., etc., etc. There are hundreds of such excuses, none of which matter much in the final analysis.

Forget all such self-justification and rationalization. Just kneel down before God and openly and honestly admit that what you did was wrong. Open your heart to your Father and commit yourself completely to him: "Dear Father, what I did was wrong, and I recognize that I have sinned. I make no excuses, but with thy help, I promise that I'll never do that thing again. I will straighten out my life, and, if necessary, go to my bishop and seek his help! From now on I pledge that I will be obedient! Please help me now to earn thy forgiveness!"

To really commit oneself and to really mean it is the beginning of repentance. Our Savior's great commitment came in the Garden of Gethsemane as he suffered in agony of spirit and shed great drops of blood in that garden. It was a time of terrible trial for him! You will remember that Jesus asked that the cup might pass from him and that some other way might be found for him. Prior to this experience, he had always had ready communication with his Heavenly Father, but now he not only felt, but indeed really was, left all alone. It was as though the heavens over his head were made of brass. He couldn't get through! So he continued to struggle in prayer and suffered horribly under the strain. It is true that he added these words, "Nevertheless not my will, but thine, be done." (Luke

22:42.) In spite of this pledge to his Heavenly Father, again and yet again he pled with his Father that the cup might pass and that some other path might be found. There was no answer to his request, and his soul filled with anguish. But the third time when he said, "Thy will be done," it was said in a different tone. This time he really *meant* it.

He realized there *was* no other way, and he fully committed himself to do whatever he had been appointed to do. He was now willing! Though it cost him tremendous suffering, he made up his mind and committed himself to be obedient in every particular, regardless of cost and suffering. It was then that the angels came to minister to him and strengthen him for his coming ordeal. That commitment made his sacrifice on the cross bearable. Such a similar struggle may cost you agony of mind and soul as well, but it will also make the repentance possible and bearable for you.

One thing we should remember is that the Lord does not punish us for our sins. He simply withholds his blessings and we punish ourselves. The scriptures tell us again and again that the wicked are punished by the wicked. A simple illustration can show how easily that is done. If Mother tells me not to touch a hot stove because it will burn and hurt me, she is only stating the law. If I should forget or deliberately touch that hot stove, I would be burned. I could cry and complain of my hurts, but who would be punishing me? Would it be Mother — or the hot stove? I would be punishing myself. Even after my finger healed, I would have to remember the law, for every time I would touch that hot stove I would be burned, again and again, until I could learn to obey the law. It was and is the law, and justice would have to be done. This illustration, however, disregards the important element of mercy.

REPAY YOUR DEBT

The second step in the process of repentance is to "give again that which you have robbed." In other words, you must restore or pay back that which you have taken. If you have stolen money or goods, it is relatively easy for you to repay—even to repay sizable amounts with time. But what if you have robbed a person of virtue? Is there anything you can do, of yourself, to restore virtue? Even if you gave your very life, could that restore virtue? No, but—perish the thought—does that then mean it is useless to attempt restitution by significant good works or that your sin is unforgivable? No! Jesus Christ can restore that virtue, and he can thus show you mercy. His repayment will satisfy justice, and he will make that payment for you *if* you will only repent.

True repentance on your part, including a change in your life-style, will enable Jesus, in mercy, to transfer your debt to him. But, as Elder Boyd K. Packer explained in his conference address of 3 April 1977, justice now requires that you repay him. Jesus has power to restore virtue and make your victim absolutely clean and holy. But, as I said, that bargain only transforms the indebtedness you have to your victim into a new indebtedness to Jesus Christ, who paid your ransom. How can you ever repay your Savior such a great price?

This may appear to you to be a new doctrine, but it is reasonable and consistent with the following scripture from Mosiah. I am grateful for the Book of Mormon, which explains how we *can* repay Jesus Christ for his great mercy

17

to us. His sacrifice atoned even for our personal sins and makes mercy available to you and to me. King Benjamin may have explained how repayment is possible: "And behold, I tell you these things that ye may learn wisdom; that ye may learn that when ye are in the service of your fellow beings ye are only in the service of your God." (Mosiah 2:17.)

This service to others can include significant good works that could compensate Jesus for his restitution made for us. God's work and glory is to redeem his children. If we participate in this redemptive service, he pays us in blessings for which we qualify by that service. What this scripture then means is that you can repay Jesus for his mercy to you by being kind, thoughtful, considerate, and helpful to those around you. By such service to others, you can gradually pay back your indebtedness to your Savior. You can put the evil you have done out of your mind by charitable service to others.

As you begin to repay your debt through service to your family, neighbors, and friends, the painful elements of your sin will gradually fade from your mind. They will no longer fill your soul with anxiety and concern, nor will you be plagued by worries over previous transgressions. Instead of being filled with vain regrets over past deeds that are already done, events you are powerless to change, you will now be so busy doing good deeds for others that you will not have a desire to sin or disobey, nor to recall past sin or disobedience. You will be helpful and considerate of everyone you meet. You will develop a loving personality and be accepted and appreciated by your associates. But as long as you dwell on sin or evil and refuse to forgive yourself, you will be subject to return again to

18

that sin. If you turn from your problems and sins and put them behind you in both thought and action, you can concentrate on good and positive things. You will thus become fully engaged in good causes. Sin will no longer be such a temptation for you.

Jesus himself said of those who attain his presence in the celestial kingdom that he would put his sheep on his right hand but place the goats to his left: "Then shall the King say unto them on his right hand, Come, ye blessed of my Father, inherit the kingdom prepared for you from the foundation of the world: For I was an hungred, and ye gave me meat; I was thirsty, and ye gave me drink; I was a stranger, and ye took me in; naked, and ye clothed me; I was sick, and ye visited me; I was in prison, and ye came unto me.

"Then shall the righteous answer him, saying, Lord, when saw we thee an hungred, and fed thee? or thirsty, and gave thee drink? When saw we thee a stranger, and took thee in? or naked, and clothed thee? Or when saw we thee sick, or in prison, and came unto thee?

"And the King shall answer and say unto them, Verily I say unto you, Inasmuch as ye have done it unto one of the *least* of these my brethren, ye have done it unto me.

"Then shall he say also unto them on the left hand, Depart from me, ye cursed, into everlasting fire, prepared for the devil and his angels; For I was an hungred, and ye gave me no meat; I was thirsty, and ye gave me no drink; I was a stranger, and ye took me not in; naked, and ye clothed me not; sick, and in prison, and ye visited me not.

"Then shall they also answer him, saying, Lord, when saw we thee an hungred, or athirst, or a stranger, or naked, or sick, or in prison, and did not minister unto thee?

19

"Then shall he answer them, saying, Verily I say unto you, Inasmuch as ye did it not to one of the least of these, ye did it not to me. And these shall go away into everlasting punishment; but the righteous into life eternal." (Matthew 25:34–46; italics added.)

In service to others, you can repay your Savior for his mercies and blessings unto you and repay him at least in part for his atonement for you. Jesus can and will lift all burdens from your soul if you will only *shube,* or turn from sin back to God.

It stands to reason that the more serious the sin, the longer it takes to complete the repayment. If you work at repayment daily over the years, even very great sins you may have committed can eventually be repaid, and you can then stand blameless before your Savior. Remember that Church leaders can forgive you for your sins against the Church, but final forgiveness for sin has to come from the Great Judge on the day of reckoning when each of us must give an account of our lives.

It takes time for repentance to be final. An injury to the soul is similar to an injury to the body. Just as it takes time for a wound in the body to heal, so it also takes time for a wound of the soul to heal. The deeper the cut in the body, the longer it takes to heal, and if broken bones are involved, that healing process is extended. If I cut myself, for example, the wound will gradually heal and scab over. But as it heals, it begins to itch, and if I scratch at the itching scab, it will take longer to heal, for the wound will open up again. But there is a greater danger. Because of the bacteria on my fingers as I scratch the scab, the wound may become infected, and I can poison the wound and can lose that part of my body and eventually even my life!

20

Allow injuries to follow their prescribed healing course, or, if serious, see a doctor for skilled help. So it is with injuries to the soul. Allow the injury to follow its prescribed healing course without scratching it through vain regrets. If it is serious, go to your bishop and get skilled help. It may hurt as he disinfects the wound and sews the flesh together, but it will heal properly that way. Don't hurry or force it, but be patient with yourself and with your thoughts. Be active with positive and righteous thoughts and deeds. Then the wound will heal properly, and you will become happy and productive again.

FORSAKE YOUR SINS

Now we come to the third step of repentance, which is to "walk in the statutes of life, without committing iniquity." In other words, we must forsake our sins, one by one, and *never* repeat them. When we do this in sincerity and with honesty of heart, the Lord has said through his prophets:

To Ezekiel: "None [not even one] of his sins that he hath committed shall be mentioned unto him; he hath done that which is lawful and right; he shall surely live." (33:16.)

To Isaiah: "I, even I, am he that blotteth out thy transgressions for mine own sake, and will not remember thy sins." (43:25.)

To Joseph Smith: "Behold, he who has repented of his sins, the same is forgiven, and I, the Lord, remember them no more." (D&C 58:42.)

But how do we know if a man or a woman has repented of his or her sins? The Lord has even answered that question: "By this ye may know if a man repenteth of his sins —

behold, he will confess them and forsake them." (D&C 58:43.)

Naturally, that confession which precedes repentance should be to a bishop or stake president who has authority to forgive sins. Confessions to others, particularly confessions repeated again and again in open meetings, as is sometimes done, only demean both the confessor and the hearer. But the final step of repentance in forsaking sin means that you do not repeat that transgression again.

How grateful we should be for a kind, wise, loving Savior who will help us overcome our faults, our mistakes, our sins. He understands us and is sympathetic to the fact that we must face temptations. He is also merciful and has provided a way so that we can apply these principles of repentance in our lives and thus escape the bondage of pain, sorrow, suffering, and despair that comes from disobedience, either conscious or unconscious. After all is said and done, we *are* his sons and his daughters, and he loves each of us dearly. For those who understand its true meaning, repentance becomes a beautiful word and a marvelous refuge.

GOD'S PLAN OF HAPPINESS

ELDER NEAL A. MAXWELL

The Lord has described his plan of redemption as the Plan of Happiness. (See Alma 42:8, 16.) Indeed, it is, but none of us is likely to be a stranger to sorrow.

Conversationally, we reference this great design almost too casually at times; we even sketch its rude outlines on chalkboards and paper as if it were the floor plan for an addition to one's house. However, when we really take time to ponder the Plan, it is breathtaking and overpowering! Indeed, I, for one, cannot decide which creates in me the most awe—its very vastness or its intricate, individualized detail.

The vastness of it all is truly overwhelming. We are living on a small planet which is part of a very modest solar system, which, in turn, is located at the outer edge of the awesome Milky Way galaxy. If we were sufficiently distant from the stunning Milky Way, it would be seen as but another bright dot among countless other bright dots in space, all of which could cause us to conclude, comparatively, "that man is nothing." (Moses 1:10.)

Yet we are rescued by such reassuring realities as that God knows and loves each of us—personally and perfectly.

23

Hence, there is incredible intimacy in the vastness of it all. Are not the very hairs of one's head numbered? Is not the fall of each sparrow noticed? (See Matt. 10:29–30.) Has Jesus not borne, and therefore does He not know, our sins, sicknesses, and infirmities? (See Alma 7:11–12.)

Furthermore, the eventual purpose of it all is centered not on some other cosmic concern but on us—"to bring to pass the immortality and eternal life of man." (Moses 1:39.) President Brigham Young said there are millions of earths like this one so that certain planets, as Isaiah said, are formed to be inhabited (see Isa. 45:18) as God's plan of salvation is executed and reexecuted! How glorious is our God! Truly, as the Psalmist said, "We are the people of his pasture, and the sheep of his hand." (Ps. 95:7.)

Has he not even told us that his "course is one eternal round"? (D&C 3:2.) Are we not also given intriguing intimations such as how "planets . . . move in their times and seasons" and how "all these kingdoms, and the inhabitants thereof" are to know the joy of seeing the countenance of the Lord—"every kingdom in its hour, and in its time, and in its season"? (D&C 88:42–43, 61.) In fact, has not the Almighty Father, who oversees it all, shared with us almost more than we can comprehend about his work? But we can understand enough to trust God regarding that which we do not understand.

Even so, since God is so serious about our joy, can we be less than serious? Can we safely postpone striving to become like him? Since there can be no true joy for us apart from doing his work, can we risk being diverted by other chores? Dare we stop short of enduring well to the end? Can we not be thankful for a purposeful life even when we have a seemingly purposeless day? Should we not be grateful for God's plan for us even when certain of our own plans for ourselves go awry?

Of course, this grand plan and design for our happiness is not something that exists merely to strike awe in us or to evoke gasps of gladness. It does not exist apart from us either, but completely involves us — painfully at times and happily at other times — but relentlessly always.

This plan is underscored by a deep, divine determination, and "there is nothing that the Lord thy God shall take in his heart to do but what he will do it." (Abr. 3:17.) Once the plan became operational (and it was with our enthusiastic consent, by the way), it could not be altered just because you and I (in the midst of an otherwise good life) might have a difficult day or a soul-stretching season in our lives. Such were clearly foreseen by him, and long ago we were deemed, if obedient, adequate to meet all such challenges. Yes, we will often feel inadequate, but fortunately he knows us far better than we know ourselves.

Let us, therefore, feast upon a few of the gospel truths that pertain to Father's Plan of Happiness. The implications for this, our second estate, are many, once we realize this life is (1) a divinely designated proving ground (see Abr. 3:25); (2) a circumstance in which those who triumph overcome by faith that is deliberately tried (see D&C 76:53); and (3) an unusual environment featuring, among other things, a dimension called time (see Alma 40:8).

It seems clear (not only scripturally but logically) that this second estate could not include either the direct memories or the reference experiences of our first estate. If such were to impinge overmuch upon this second estate, our mortality would not be a true proving ground.

In like manner, the veil also stands between us and

that which lies ahead, our third and everlasting estate. If, for instance, our association with resurrected beings in this second estate were the order of the day, if they walked with us in the marketplace and conversed with us in the Gospel Doctrine class, no true growth or test, as were envisioned, could really occur.

Therefore, much as we might like to have the curtains parted so that (not only "on a clear day" but all the time) we could see forever, thereby knowing the circumstances, events, and challenges that lie ahead of us—those things are, for the most part, kept carefully from us. Indeed, it appears that such understanding is usually given only to those individuals who have progressed sufficiently spiritually, that they can be trusted with such knowledge, because it will not distract or divert them or cause them to slacken.

To give people spiritual knowledge—in advance of their capacity to understand it or to apply it—is no favor. (See Matt. 7:6.) Even yesterday's righteous experience does not guarantee us against tomorrow's relapse. A few who have had supernal spiritual experiences have later fallen. Hence, enduring well to the end assumes real significance, and we are at risk till the end!

Thus, the Lord has created this planet—our customized schoolhouse—so carefully in order that it would be environmentally inhabitable. Likewise, God has carefully designed the curriculum to be used therein to be strictly consistent with his proving purposes. Walter Bagehot put it well: "*If* the universe were to be incessantly expressive and incessantly communicative, morality would be impossible: we should live under the unceasing pressure of a supernatural interference, which would give us selfish motives for doing everything, which would menace us with supernatural punishment if we left anything undone; we should be living in a chastising machine . . . the life which we lead and were meant to lead would be impossible. . . . True virtue would become impossible. . . . A sun that shines and a rain which falls equally on the evil and on the good, are essential to morality in a being free like man and created as man was." (*The Works of Walter Bagehot,* ed. Forrest Morgan, Hartford, Connecticut: The Travelers Insurance Company, 1889, 2:313.)

Thus, while there is a spiritual ecology (and when we violate it we pay a certain price), the costs or consequences are not always immediate nor externally visible. Thieves are not always brought immediately to justice. A child-abusing parent is not at once restrained. So, in a hundred ways that could be illustrated, the outward judgment of God does not immediately fall upon an erring individual so that this second estate may be a true proving ground; and also, mercifully, so we can, if we will, know the refreshment and renewal of repentance. Without repentance the past would forever hold the future hostage!

This mortal condition affords to all but those who die young (but who die unto the Lord) options to choose among, time enough to choose, and the opportunity to experience the consequences of our choices—"according to the flesh." (Alma 7:12.) So it is that most mortals live and learn (or fail to learn) "in process of time." (Moses 7:21, 68.)

Since, for example, almost all individuals have a tendency to abuse power and authority—not just a few, not even a mere majority—how are the relevant lessons about the righteous use of power to be learned except in this

27

laboratory-of-life setting? Could we have truly experienced the risks and opportunities of power merely by attending some pointed lectures or doing some directed reading during our first estate? Was it not necessary to experience, "according to the flesh," what it is like to be on the receiving end of unrighteous dominion? And the necessity of repentance when one has been on the giving end? The general absence, for instance, on the human political scene of attributes such as genuine humility, mercy, and meekness is a grim reminder, again and again, of how essential these qualities are to the governance of self or a nation. (See D&C 121:34–44.)

In some respects, it is easier to govern a whole people than oneself. Of one ancient political leader, it is candidly recorded: "And he did do justice unto the people, but not unto himself because of his many whoredoms; wherefore he was cut off from the presence of the Lord." (Ether 10:11.) One can cater to mortal constituencies but lose the support of the one Elector who matters!

We know that God's "word of power" brings entire new worlds into being and causes others to pass away. (See Moses 1:35–38.) But the powers of heaven cannot be handled or controlled except upon the basis of righteousness. (See D&C 121:36.) Real righteousness, therefore, cannot be a superficial, ritualistic thing. It must arise out of the deepest convictions of the soul, not out of a desire merely to "go along" with the Heavenly Regime simply because that's how things are done! God's power—unlike mortal power—is accessed only by those who have developed, to a requisite degree, God's attributes.

Jesus counseled us, too, concerning materialism and "the deceitfulness of riches" (Matt. 13:22), and of how hard it is for those who trust in riches and materialism to enter into the kingdom of God. (See Luke 18:24.) Another of those scalding but divine generalizations! The relevant mortal experiences permit (but do not guarantee) that we will learn about what should come first in life. Can those who are diverted by riches or the search for riches and thus fail to discern the real purposes of life be safely trusted with greater dominions that call for even greater discernment? "And he that overcometh, and keepeth my works unto the end, to him will I give power over the nations." (Rev. 2:26.) Could we truly appreciate the supremacy of spiritual things without experiencing the limitations of material things? Not in just one brief encounter, but day by day?

Since "he that hath no rule over his own spirit is like a city that is broken down, and without walls" (Prov. 25:28), how could we learn to govern ourselves without the specific opportunities for growth and failure that daily life affords? In fact, is not managing life's *little* challenges so often the *big* challenge? Those who wait for the single, spectacular, final exam are apt to flunk the daily quizzes!

We are to strive to become perfect, even as our Father in Heaven is perfect. (See Matt. 5:48.) But this is not just generalized goodness; rather, it is the attainment of specific attributes. So it is that, if God intends to use us (and he does), he must school us so that we emulate his attributes and function in harmony with the laws of his universe while yet in this "proving ground." We do not fully know why our obedience in the *here and now* is so crucial, but it is no doubt bound up in our *usefulness* and *happiness* in the *there and then!*

Moreover, even when we fail to develop an eternal

29

attribute sufficiently, our mortal experiences will never-theless have shown us just how precious that attribute is. How much easier, later on, to accept with appreciation the righteous dominion of those who have so progressed. Again, could such appreciation and acceptance have been generated in the abstract?

We are even reassured that our mortal performance will be judged according to what has been allotted to us and how we use our talents within that allocation. (See Alma 29:3, 6; Matt. 25:14–30.) We will not be able to invoke, justifiably, either deprivational or circumstantial evidence in our own behalf later on to show that we were dealt with unjustly. The record will be clear! Perhaps that stark reality will contribute to the response of those who, at judgment time, will wish to be buried under mountains and rocks to hide them from the face of God! (See Rev. 6:16.)

Thus, the whole mortal schooling process has been so carefully structured to achieve results that could be achieved in "no other way." (Hel. 5:9.) We can come to know the Lord as our loving, tutoring Father and God — but not as a policeman posted at every intersection of our lives!

Hence, our submissiveness to the Lord must be the real thing, not the equivalent of obeying the speed limit only as long as the highway patrolman is there in his pace-car. Indeed, awaiting full development is our willingness "to submit to all things which the Lord seeth fit to inflict upon [us], even as a child doth submit to his father." (Mosiah 3:19.) This is a sobering gospel truth about sub-missiveness. It is a wintry declaration. This truth is not likely to evoke from us an "Oh, goodie" response.

During our schooling in submissiveness, we will see

the visible crosses some carry, but other crosses will go unseen. A few individuals may appear to have no trial at all, which, if it were so, would be a trial in itself. Indeed, if our souls had rings, as do trees, to measure the years of greatest personal growth, the wide rings would likely reflect the years of greatest moisture—but from tears, not rainfall.

Most of our suffering comes from sin and stupidity; it is, nevertheless, very real, and growth can occur with real repentance. But the highest source of suffering appears to be reserved for the innocent who undergo divine tutorial training.

Thus we see how gospel truths concerning the plan of salvation are much more than a "tourist guide" for the second estate; they include a degree of understanding of what Paul called "the deep things of God." (1 Cor. 2:10.) In our moments of deep anguish, suffering, and bewilderment—in those moments when we ask in faith for certain outcomes and are refused, because to give them to us would not be "right" (3 Ne. 18:20)—then our faith is either deepened or slackened.

Yes, even in our prayers, we can, unintentionally, ask "amiss." (2 Ne. 4:35.) No wonder humility is such an everlasting virtue. For us to accept God's no as an affirmative indication of his love—rather than a lack thereof—and as a signal that we have asked amiss, this is true humility!

How often have you and I in our provincialism prayed to see ahead and, mercifully, have been refused, lest our view of the present be blurred? How many times have we been blessed by *not* having our prayers answered, at least according to the specifications set forth in our petitions? How many times have frustrating, even gruelling, expe-

31

riences from which we have sought relief turned out, later on, to have been part of a necessary preparation that led to much more happiness? "And now when Alma heard this, . . . he beheld that their afflictions had truly humbled them, and that they were *in a preparation to hear the word.*" (Alma 32:6; italics added.)

How many times have we impatiently expressed our discontent with seemingly ordinary and routine circumstances that were divinely designed, shaping circumstances for which, later on, we were very grateful? Alas, have there perhaps not also been those times when we have been grumpy with God or, unlike Job, even "charged God foolishly"? (Job 1:22.) How many times, naively, have we vigorously protested while on our way to a blessing?

Therefore, our faith in and thanksgiving for Heavenly Father, so far as this mortal experience is concerned, consists not simply of a faith and gladness that he exists, but also includes faith and thanksgiving for his tutoring of us to aid our acquisition of needed attributes and experiences while we are in mortality. We trust not only the Designer but also his design of life itself—including our portion thereof! Our response to the realities of the plan should not be resignation or shoulder-shrugging fatalism—but reverential acceptance! If, at times, we wonder, we will also know what it is to be filled with wonderment.

Why should it surprise us, by the way, that life's most demanding tests as well as life's most significant opportunities for growth usually occur within marriage and the family? How can revolving-door relationships, by contrast, be a real test of our capacity to love? Is being courteous, one time, to the stranger on the bus as difficult as being courteous to a family member who is competing for the bathroom morning after morning? Does fleeting disappointment with a fellow office worker compare to the betrayal of a spouse? Does a raise in pay even approach the lift we receive from rich family life?

Besides, even the most seemingly ordinary life contains more than enough clinical opportunities for our personal growth and development. By the way, while mortality features "an opposition in all things" (2 Ne. 2:11), we need feel no obligation to supply opposition or to make life difficult. Sufficient unto each situation are the challenges thereof!

Should it surprise us that in striving to acquire and develop celestial attributes, the greater the interpersonal proximity, the greater the challenge? Is not patience, for instance, best developed among those with whom we interface incessantly? The same is true with any of the other eternal attributes! Hence the high adventure of marriage and family life—and why it is that so many run away from these challenges, thinking they can avoid having to confront themselves by losing themselves in other endeavors or life-styles!

Is not gospel perspective about the plan of salvation so precious, therefore, in the midst of "all these things" which are designed to give us experience? Yes, let us be filled with an attitude of thanksgiving in our journey homeward, but not become too comfortable here, as C. S. Lewis observed: "Our Father [in Heaven] refreshes us on the journey [through life] with some pleasant inns, but [he] will not encourage us to mistake them for home." (*The Problem of Pain*, New York: Macmillan, 1967, p. 103.)

Nor should the praise and positions accorded to us by men in the second estate come to matter too much either, as an aging but articulate Malcolm Muggeridge observed on his own mortal journey: "Now, the prospect of death overshadows all others. I am like a man on a sea voyage nearing his destination. When I embarked I worried about having a cabin with a porthole, whether I should be asked to sit at the captain's table, who were the more attractive and important passengers. All such considerations become pointless when I shall soon be disembarking." (*Things Past*, ed. Ian Hunter, New York: William Morrow and Company, Inc., 1979, p. 166.)

And when the gossamer veil called time is "too much with us," let us recall that, ere long, time will be no more. Time is measured only to man anyway. (See Rev. 10:6; Alma 40:8; D&C 84:100.) Meanwhile, let us make allowance for the rapidity with which time seems to pass, especially when we are happy. Jacob found it so: "And Jacob served seven years for Rachel; and they seemed unto him but a few days, for the love he had to her." (Gen. 29:20.) On such a scale, each of us has but a few days left in mortality!

As men and women of Christ, we can be led by him through this second estate, in the words of Helaman, "in a strait and narrow course across that everlasting gulf of misery which is prepared to engulf the wicked—and land their souls, yea, their immortal souls, at the right hand of God in the kingdom of heaven, to sit down with Abraham, and Isaac, and with Jacob, and with all our holy fathers, to go no more out." (Hel. 3:29–30.)

"*To go no more out*"! An intriguing promise! For the busy, for those ceaselessly on the move, for the homeless, for the lonely, and for widows and widowers—and for others of us who will become such—does not the prospect of this homecoming in such grand and everlasting circumstances warm the soul? Not, of course, that life hereafter is to consist of unending repose. Rather, for those who attain the presence of God, "to go no more out" — nowhere is really out of his presence, and now is forever! As time is no more, likewise space will shrink irrevocably. For all we know, the speed of light may prove too slow to do some of what must be done.

No wonder it is called the Plan of Happiness! No wonder the divine and prophetic exhortations to us are so straightforward and repetitive! No wonder we should be so thankful, so everlastingly thankful! Is God's Plan of Happiness not a most fundamental cause for thanksgiving this day and always?

THE REWARDS
OF REPENTANCE

ELDER F. BURTON HOWARD

Picture in your mind two crystal goblets. They differ in size and shape. They are both of good quality and have been well used. One has been carefully kept in a china cupboard. It is clean and polished. It is warm and inviting in appearance. It sparkles in the light and is filled with clear water.

The other glass is coated with grime. It has not been in the dishpan for a long time. It has been used for purposes other than those for which it was made. Most recently it has been left outside in the weather and has served as a flowerpot. Although the flower is gone, it is still filled with dirt. It is dull and unbecoming in the light.

Is not each of us like a crystal glass? We vary in size and shape. Some of us radiate a special spirit. Some are dull and uninviting. Some fill the measure of their creation. Others do not. Each is filled with the accumulated experiences or debris of a lifetime.

Some contain mostly good things—clean thoughts, faith, and Christian service. These hold wisdom and peace. Others enclose dark and secret things. Over time they have filled with unclean thoughts, selfishness, and sloth. They often hold doubt, contention, and unrest. Many know they are not living up to their potential but for various reasons have procrastinated making changes in their lives. Some long for they know not what and spend their lives in a haphazard pursuit of happiness.

These, in a way, are like the crystal goblet that spent part of its existence filled with dirt. They sense that there is a higher purpose to things. They become dissatisfied and begin to search for meaning. First they look outside themselves. They sample the pleasures of the world. As they do, they discover, much as did the snail who set out to look for its house, that after arriving at wherever they were going, they are no closer than before to the object of their search.

Ultimately, they look within. They have really known all the time that this is where to find peace. Sin, you see, is not just a state of mind. Wickedness never was and never will be happiness. (See Alma 41:10.) They discover that if they are not righteous, they can never be happy. (See 2 Ne. 2:13.) They resolve to change. Then they are confronted, figuratively, with the problem of how to turn a weathered flowerpot into a sparkling crystal goblet. Questions are asked: Can I ever be forgiven? Is it really worth the effort? Where do I begin?

In the case of the glass, it is easy to understand what to do. We begin by recognizing a better use for the crystal. A convenient place for dumping unwanted contents is selected. The dirt is left there. The goblet is carefully washed with high-quality detergent to remove the stains and residue. It is lovingly polished and placed once again in the company of the other crystal glasses in the china cupboard. It is put back into use and cared for regularly.

There is a similar process whereby men and women are purified. The misuse of their lives is forgotten, and they are renewed and changed. This principle, of course, is repentance. When accompanied by authorized baptism, it provides not only an initial cleansing but an ongoing remission of sins as well. Participating in this purifying process is perhaps the most thrilling and important thing we can ever do. It has far-reaching, even eternal, consequences. Of more immediate interest, however, the rewards of repentance are peace and forgiveness in this present life.

Let me illustrate what all of this means. When I was a bishop, I once spoke to a group of young men. I don't remember now exactly what was said, except that near the end I made the statement that no one, but no one, present had done anything for which he could not be forgiven. After the meeting was over, one of them came up to me and said, "I just have to talk to you." Inasmuch as I soon had another appointment, I asked if it could wait or if someone else could answer his question. He replied that he had already waited many years and that it was very important to him. So taking advantage of the few minutes available, we found a little unused classroom, went in, and closed the door. "Did you really mean it? Did you?" he asked.

"Mean what?" I said.

"The part about how none of us had done anything that could not be forgiven," he replied.

"Of course I did," I said.

Through his tears his story came. He was of goodly parents. All his life his mother had told him that he was going on a mission. Before he turned nineteen, he was involved in serious transgression. He didn't know how to tell his parents. He knew it would break their hearts. He knew that he wasn't worthy to serve a mission. In desperation, he began to look for an excuse not to go. He decided to take up smoking. He felt that his father could understand that better and would not probe for the real reason. Smoking would hurt his parents, he rationalized, but not as deeply as the truth.

He soon found, however, that the former bishop wasn't put off by his use of tobacco. He told him to just stop it and go on a mission anyway. So to get away from the bishop, he entered the military service. There he fell under the influence of some good Latter-day Saints. He stopped smoking. He was able to avoid major temptations. He served his time, received an honorable discharge, and returned home.

There was only one problem. He felt guilty. He had run away from a mission. He had run from the Lord and sensed somehow that gnawing discontent that comes when men do not live up to the purpose of their creation.

"So there you have it," he said. "I have not sinned again. I have attended my meetings. I keep the Word of Wisdom. Why is it that life seems empty? Why do I feel somehow that the Lord is displeased with me? Tell me, bishop, how can I know for sure that I have been forgiven?"

"Tell me what you know about repentance," I said.

He had obviously done some reading on the subject. He spoke of recognition, remorse, and restitution. He had resolved never to sin again.

"Let's see just how those principles apply to you," I said. "Let's begin with recognition. What is the best indicator that someone recognizes he has done wrong?"

"He will admit it" was his reply.

"To whom?" I asked.

He was thoughtful. "To himself, I guess."

"Men sometimes view themselves in a most favorable light," I said. "Wouldn't better evidence of awareness of wrongdoing be to tell someone else?"

"Yes, of course," he answered.

"Who else?" I insisted.

"Why, the person wronged," he said, "and . . . and maybe the bishop."

"Have you done this?" I asked.

"Not until now," he replied. "I never told it all to anyone but you."

"Maybe that is why you have not ever felt completely forgiven," I responded.

He didn't say much.

"Let's look at the next step," I said. "What does it mean to feel remorse?"

"It means to be sorry," he answered.

"Are you sorry?" I asked.

"Oh yes," he said. "I feel as if I have wasted half my life." And his eyes filled again with tears.

"How sorry should you be?"

He looked puzzled. "What do you mean?"

I said, "Well, in order to be forgiven, a transgressor must experience godly sorrow. (See 2 Cor. 7:10.) He must have anguish of soul and genuine regret. This sorrow must be strong enough and long enough to motivate the additional processes of repentance, or it is not deep enough. Regret must be great enough so as to bring forth a changed person. That person must demonstrate that he is different

40

than before by doing different and better things. Have you been sorry enough?" I asked again.

He hesitated. "I've changed," he said. "I'm not the same as I was before. I keep the commandments now. I would like somehow to make it up to my parents. I have prayed for forgiveness. I apologized to the person I wronged. I realize the seriousness of what I have done. I would give anything if it hadn't happened. Maybe I haven't been as good as I could be, but I don't know what else to do. But I didn't ever confess to anyone."

I said, "I think after this meeting we can say you have even done that."

Then he said, "But after all of that, how can I ever know the Lord has really forgiven me?"

"That is the easy part," I replied. "When you have fully repented, you feel an inner peace. You know somehow you are forgiven because the burden you have carried for so long all of a sudden isn't there anymore. It is *gone* and *you know* it is gone."

He seemed doubtful still.

"I wouldn't be surprised," I said, "if when you leave this room, you discover that you have left much of your concern in here. If you have fully repented, the relief and the peace you feel will be so noticeable that it will be a witness to you that the Lord has forgiven you. If not today, I think it will happen soon."

I was late for my meeting. I opened the door and we went out together. I didn't know if we would ever meet again. The following Sunday evening, I received a telephone call at my home. It was from the young man.

"Bishop, how did you know?"

"How did I know what?" I asked.

41

"How did you know I would feel good about myself for the first time in five years?"

"Because the Lord promised he would remember no more," I said. (See Heb. 8:12.)

Then came the question: "Do think the Church could use a twenty-four-year-old missionary? If they could, I would sure like to go."

Well, that young man was like one of the glasses we spoke about. He had been out in the world and was partially filled with the wrong things. He was not content. Sin had clouded his vision and interfered with his potential. Until he could find a way to repent, he could never become what he knew he should be. It took time to change. It took prayer. It took effort, and it took help.

My young friend discovered that repentance is often a lonely, silent struggle. It is not a once-in-a-lifetime thing; rather, it lasts a lifetime. As President Stephen L Richards once said, it is an "ever-recurring acknowledgement of weakness and error and [a] seeking and living for the higher and better." (Conference Report, April 1956, p. 91.)

This young man came to know that repentance is not a free gift. Just as faith without works is dead (see James 2:17), so repentance, too, demands much. It is not for the fainthearted or the lazy. It requires a complete turning away from wrongdoing and a set of new works or doings that produce a new heart and a different man. Repentance means work. It is not just recognizing the wrong or knowing what should be done. It is not "a cycle of sinning and repenting and sinning again." (Hugh B. Brown, *Eternal Quest*, Salt Lake City: Bookcraft, 1956, p. 102.) It is not only remorse; rather, it is an eternal principle, which, when properly applied over sufficient time, always results in renewal, cleansing, and change.

The young man we have spoken about discovered that where sin is so serious as to jeopardize one's fellowship in the Church, the sinner must be willing to submit to the jurisdiction and judgment of the person who holds the custody of his Church membership and request forgiveness of him as well.

Most important of all, he learned that repentance is an indispensable counterpart to free agency. Free agency in the plan of salvation contemplates that men and women are free to choose the direction of their lives for themselves. Repentance means that as imperfect beings sometimes make imperfect decisions, they may correct their course. By following the rules of repentance, and through the atonement of Jesus Christ, mistakes don't count. The Lord agrees to "remember no more." (Heb. 8:12.) Because of the miraculous gift of forgiveness, transgressions are forgiven—*and forgotten*. Men can be cleansed and return to the path of purpose and progress and peace.

By repenting, my young friend became a new person. He was born again of the Spirit. He came to understand for himself, and that is the important thing, the meaning of the Savior's words: "Come unto me, all ye that labour and are heavy laden, and I will give you rest." (Matt. 11:28.)

BEGINNING AGAIN

ELDER HUGH W. PINNOCK

I have watched with deep concern a number of instances that have unfolded into frustration, heartache, and seeming hopelessness. I write therefore to those who suffer with pain and who are aching with grief, anger, and guilt. What I write applies also to those who will yet pass through periods of anguish and difficulty.

When we were little, many of us repeated a verse that began:

> *I wish that there were some wonderful place*
> *Called the Land of Beginning Again,*
> *Where all our mistakes, and all our heartaches*
> *And all of our poor selfish grief*
> *Could be dropped like a shabby old coat at the door,*
> *And never be put on again.*
> *(Louise Fletcher, "The Land of Beginning Again.")*

The "Land of Beginning Again" does not exist in a geographical location, but there is a specific spiritual position from which we can all start anew, shedding our pains, guilt, and sorrows. Let us travel there this morning.

The ancient prophet Jeremiah was in his house one

day and heard the word of the Lord saying: "Arise, and go down to the potter's house, and, behold, he wrought a work on the wheels. And the vessel that he made of clay was marred in the hand of the potter: so he made it again another vessel, as seemed good to the potter to make it. Then the word of the Lord came again to me, saying, O house of Israel, cannot I do with you as this potter? . . . Behold, as the clay is in the potter's hand, so are ye in mine hand, O house of Israel." (Jer. 18:2–6.)

The Lord explained to Jeremiah that when we make mistakes, as ancient Israel was making, we can take what we have marred and begin again. The potter did not give up and throw the clay away, just because he had made a mistake. And we are not to feel hopeless and reject ourselves. Yes, our task is to overcome our problems, take what we have and are, and start again.

Perhaps you have sinned in ways that are significant, embarrassing, and destructive. Yet, by following the simple instruction given by the Master, you can talk with your bishop, when necessary, and begin again as a renewed person.

Or maybe you have placed your money in an investment that has proven to be unwise or unprofitable. Now is an opportunity for you to begin again. Don't let a mistake injure you twice as it does if you harbor a past wrong or injustice and let your anger destroy you.

Perhaps you have hurt others, bringing pain, fear, and heartache to them. Now is the time to go and express sorrow for what you have done, beg their forgiveness, and whenever possible, restore that which has been taken. When? Now! It is God's design that we pay our obligations. In the Doctrine and Covenants he said, "Behold it is my will that you *shall* pay all your debts." (D&C 104:78; italics added.)

At the peak of its power, the Greek Empire sprawled from the Mediterranean Basin on the west to what is present-day India on the east. Through military strength, the Greeks had conquered countless city-states and nations. They honored their bravest men, but also hallowed the site at which the tide of each battle turned. They marked that single spot on the plain of conflict where a small victory had made the ultimate triumph inevitable. At that place, they pushed a piece of stone or a pile of captured weapons into an upright position. They called the marker a trophy. In the language of the ancient Greeks, the word *trophy* meant "a turning."

Is now a time for a trophy in your life? In the battles you are fighting, should you erect a monument to show that you have turned, that your life will be different now?

Remember, not all problems keel over as Goliath did before David. Not all battles end as dramatically as the one fought at Cumorah. Not all miracles are as immediate as when Joseph Smith blessed the sick on the banks of the Mississippi River. But problems do go away, battles are won, and miracles do occur in the lives of us all. In Deuteronomy 7:22 the Lord described his battle plan for purifying Israel in this way: "And the Lord thy God will put out those nations before thee by little and little." Victory often does come little by little.

Let me suggest the steps necessary to turn our lives in a new direction. The business of life is to climb higher. The divine step is to repent. Repentance means to find a better way and to follow it.

First, eliminate from our thinking and our vocabulary

the phrase *"if only* I had done something differently." *If only* Samson had known the results of his association with Delilah, he never would have made the first visit. (See Judg. 16.) *If only* Sidney Rigdon had been able to foresee his pathetic end, he might have humbled himself and stayed with the Church. *If only* the rich man could have seen beyond the grave, he might have started praying sooner, but only in hell did he become a praying man. (See Luke 16:19–25.) *If only* you had not gone on that date, or taken that trip, or made that investment, or met that person, your life might have been different.

All of us can waste precious time by saying, "What *if* I had not done something or other?" "What if" is not an appropriate question if we really want to start again. Let us face head-on where we are and where we want to be and not dwell on the "what ifs" of yesterday.

Second, do not wait till tomorrow to begin again. "Boast not thyself of to morrow; for thou knowest not what a day may bring forth." (Prov. 27:1.) *Today* is the day for each of us to erect those monuments on our own battlefields and mark the place where we began again. One of the reasons we have conferences is to learn how to be better.

Third, resolve to live the gospel of Jesus Christ in its entirety. "For you shall live by every word that proceedeth forth from the mouth of God." (D&C 84:44.) Many people live the gospel according to themselves. That is self-deception. There is only one true gospel. We may alter it or tint it with our own notions. But if we will adhere to the pure teachings of Jesus Christ, we will eliminate many of the rationalizations that lead to problems. The menu has only one entree. To pick and choose which of God's precepts to live is satanic self-centeredness. Integrity is the foundation of our life-style.

Fourth, face reality. Sometimes we wish we could fly from our troubles. King David did. He had been a good man, but he engulfed himself in great difficulties. It seemed to be more than he could bear. One day he cried, "Oh that I had wings like a dove! for then would I fly away, and be at rest." (Ps. 55:6.) His guilt-fired emotions had gained the upper hand. He wanted to get away from everything. Some try to fly away physically, and others try to do so emotionally. That does not solve problems. The only true escape route is marked with the sign "personal responsibility." Remember, the Savior said "Come unto me, all ye that labour and are heavy laden, and I will give you rest." (Matt. 11:28.) He invited us to learn of him and to take his yoke upon us. (See Matt. 11:29.)

Fifth, approach our challenges positively! Take over! Lead out! A poet wrote:

> *Never give up! If adversity presses,*
> *Providence wisely has mingled the cup,*
> *And the best counsel, in all your distresses,*
> *Is the stout watchword of "Never give up!"*
> *(Martin F. Tupper, "Never Give Up.")*

We recall with clarity these words of the Master: "Seek ye first to build up the kingdom of God, and to establish his righteousness; and all these things shall be added unto you." (JST, Matt. 6:38.) Just a few verses later, the Savior tells us, "Ask, and it shall be given you; seek, and ye shall find; knock, and it shall be opened unto you." (Matt. 7:7.)

Sixth, don't begin again partially. Be complete! Otherwise, you may be patching up an old article of clothing with a little piece of new material. The old fabric will not hold. As Jesus said, "No man putteth a piece of new cloth unto an old garment, for . . . the rent is made worse." (Matt. 9:16.) Don't patch. Begin a whole new life. The wealthy young man was unwilling to give all, to follow the Master totally, and so "he went away sorrowful" (Matt. 19:22), and was never heard from again.

Seventh, be open and candid in your relationships with others. So many of life's difficulties are brought about by being double-minded. Let us learn to say it as it is. Think of Peter's extreme discomfort when the Master addressed him after Peter had been teaching a false concept: "Thou art an offence unto me: for thou savourest not the things that be of God, but those that be of man." (Matt. 16:23.) From that moment, Peter was a greater disciple. The person who is open and honest will be vindicated. Time is his friend. Trust is his reward.

Last, and perhaps the hardest of all, forgive. Paul said, "To whom ye forgive any thing, I forgive also." (2 Cor. 2:10.) Certainly part of beginning again is to "love your enemies, do good to them which hate you, Bless them that curse you, and pray for them which despitefully use you." (Luke 6:27–28.) Paul reinforced this admonition when he said, "See that none render evil for evil unto any man; but ever follow that which is good, both among yourselves, and to all men." (1 Thes. 5:15.) Revenge has no place in the life of a person who has found the "Land of Beginning Again."

Think how young Joseph had been wronged by jealous brothers anciently. They sold him into slavery. He had every reason to seek revenge. But when circumstances joined them together again in Egypt, Joseph said, "But as for you, ye thought evil against me; but God meant it unto good, . . . to save much people." (Gen. 50:20.)

Yes, so much of heartache and grief eventually become blessings, our earthly instructions, and condition us spiritually. Even if we cannot understand the "whys" of our tribulations, we can still turn to God and rededicate our lives to his safekeeping. Yes, "he who doeth the works of righteousness shall receive his reward, even peace in this world, and eternal life in the world to come." (D&C 59:23.)

GOD'S LOVE FOR US TRANSCENDS OUR TRANSGRESSIONS

ELDER RONALD E. POELMAN

The Galilean fisherman Simon Peter, upon recognizing for the first time the divine power of Jesus, exclaimed, "Depart from me; for I am a sinful man, O Lord." (Luke 5:8.) Each one of us, at times, may feel as Peter did, conscious of our failings and uncomfortable at the thought of approaching the Lord. Transgression causes us to feel estranged from our Father in Heaven, and we feel unworthy of his love and fearful of his disapproval.

Yet, having transgressed his laws or disobeyed his commandments, we need the strengthening influence of our Father to help us overcome our weakness, to repent and become reconciled with him. Unrepented sin tends to become habitual and is frequently accompanied by a deepening sense of guilt, which may make repentance increasingly difficult. This feeling of estrangement from the Lord becomes, itself, an impediment to repentance and reconciliation with him.

Knowing we have offended our Father in Heaven, we are afraid to ask his help, feeling that we don't deserve it. Paradoxically, when we are most in need of the Lord's influence, we deserve it least. Nevertheless, in such circumstances he says to us, as Jesus said to the trembling Peter, "Fear not." (Luke 5:10.)

This message might best be illustrated through the experiences of a young couple whom I will call John and Gayle. John was a thoughtful, kind young man, affectionate, with a frank and open manner. He sincerely tried to obey the Lord's commandments and found honest contentment in the joys of family life. Gayle, his wife, was young, attractive, high-spirited, but inclined toward more worldly interests and activities. The society in which they lived was, in general, one of affluence and materialism. People seemed preoccupied with temporal gain, social status, entertainment, and self-gratification. Religious leaders were concerned about the apparent breakdown in family life and moral standards.

In the early years of their marriage, John and Gayle were blessed with children, first a boy and then a girl; but Gayle seemed uninterested in her domestic responsibilities. She longed for glamour and excitement in her life, and she was frequently away from home at parties and entertainments, not always with her husband. In her vanity, Gayle encouraged and responded to the attentions of other men until eventually she was unfaithful to her marriage vows.

Throughout, John encouraged Gayle to appreciate the joys of family life and experience the rewards of observing the laws of God. He was patient and kind, but to no avail. Shortly after the birth of a third child, a son, Gayle deserted her husband and children and joined her worldly friends in a life of self-indulgence and immorality. John, thus rejected, was humiliated and brokenhearted.

Soon, however, the glamour and excitement that had

52

attracted Gayle turned to ashes. Her so-called friends tired of her and abandoned her. Then each successive step was downward, her life becoming more and more degraded. Eventually she recognized her mistakes and realized what she had lost but could see no way back. Certainly John could not possibly love her still. She felt completely unworthy of his love and undeserving of her home and family.

Then one day, passing through the streets, John recognized Gayle. Surely he would have been justified in turning away, but he didn't. As he observed the effect of her recent life, all too evident, a feeling of compassion came over him—a desire to reach out to her. Learning that Gayle had incurred substantial debts, John repaid them and then took her home.

Soon John realized, at first with amazement, that he still loved Gayle. Out of his love for her and her willingness to change and begin anew, there grew in John's heart a feeling of merciful forgiveness, a desire to help Gayle overcome her past and to accept her again fully as his wife.

Through his personal experience there arose in John another profound awareness, a realization of the nature of God's love for us, his children. Though we disregard his counsel, break his commandments, and reject him, when we recognize our mistakes and desire to repent, he wants us to seek him out, and he will accept us.

John had been prepared, through his personal experiences, for a divine mission. Though I have taken some literary license in telling the story, it is the account, perhaps allegorical, of Hosea, prophet of the Old Testament, and his wife, Gomer. Portraying God to ancient Israel as a loving, forgiving father, Hosea foreshadowed, more than most Old Testament prophets, the spirit and message of the New Testament, the Book of Mormon, and modern revelation. In these latter days the Lord has said: "For I the Lord cannot look upon sin with the least degree of allowance; nevertheless, he that repents and does the commandments of the Lord shall be forgiven." (D&C 1:31–32.)

By disobeying the laws of God and breaking his commandments, we do offend him, we do estrange ourselves from him, and we don't deserve his help and inspiration and strength. But God's love for us transcends our transgressions.

When we disobey the laws of God, justice requires that compensation be made—a requirement that we are incapable of fulfilling. But out of his divine love for us, our Father has provided a plan and a Savior, Jesus Christ, whose redeeming sacrifice satisfies the demands of justice for us and makes possible repentance, forgiveness, and reconciliation with our Father. For indeed, "God so loved the world, that he gave his only begotten Son, that whosoever believeth in him should not perish, but have everlasting life." (John 3:16.)

We may accept this great gift through faith in Jesus Christ and repentance, followed by a covenant made with him through baptism of the water and of the Spirit. Then, each week, as we receive the sacrament, we renew our covenant that we will "always remember him and keep his commandments." The promise attached to that covenant is that we "may always have his Spirit to be with [us]." (D&C 20:77.)

Hosea's ancient message is repeated and elaborated throughout the scriptures. Through Isaiah, another Old

Testament prophet, the Lord said to his people: "Wash you, make you clean; put away the evil of your doings from before mine eyes; cease to do evil; learn to do well. . . . Come now, and let us reason together, saith the Lord: though your sins be as scarlet, they shall be as white as snow; though they be red like crimson, they shall be as wool." (Isa. 1:16–18.)

The Lord, speaking to Alma, the Nephite prophet, says: "Whosoever transgresseth against me, him shall ye judge according to the sins which he committed; and if he confess his sins before thee and me, and repenteth in the sincerity of his heart, him shall ye forgive, and I will forgive him also. Yea, and as often as my people repent will I forgive them their trespasses against me." (Mosiah 26: 29–30.)

Too often we make repentance more difficult for each other by our failure to forgive one another. However, we are admonished in modern revelation that "ye ought to forgive one another; for he that forgiveth not his brother his trespasses standeth condemned before the Lord; for there remaineth in him the greater sin. I, the Lord, will forgive whom I will forgive, but of you it is required to forgive all men." (D&C 64:9–10.) Also from modern revelation comes one of the most comforting, hopeful pronouncements ever spoken: "He who has repented of his sins, the same is forgiven, and I, the Lord, remember them no more." (D&C 58:42.)

God is our father; he loves us; his love is infinite and unconditional. His sorrow is great when we disobey his commandments and break his laws. He cannot condone our transgressions, but he loves us and wants us to return

55

to him. I know of no greater inducement to repentance and reconciliation with our Father in Heaven than an awareness of his love for us personally and individually. My hope is that such awareness may increase within each of us.

"FORGIVE THEM,
I PRAY THEE"

ELDER VAUGHN J. FEATHERSTONE

Some time ago, a young wife spoke at her husband's funeral and said, "We came to realize that unimportant things really are unimportant. When the spirit is sick, there can be no true healing, no matter how strong the physical body. If the spirit is well, then physical impairment is unimportant, regardless of the effects of a debilitating disease."

The Lord has provided the way whereby our spiritual sicknesses can be healed. In the first chapter of Isaiah, verse 18, we read, "Come now, and let us reason together, saith the Lord: though your sins be as scarlet, they shall be as white as snow; though they be red like crimson, they shall be as wool." And again, in the Doctrine and Covenants, "Nevertheless, he that repents and does the commandments of the Lord shall be forgiven." (D&C 1:32.) Also, "Behold, he who has repented of his sins, the same is forgiven, and I, the Lord, remember them no more." (D&C 58:42.)

For one to be forgiven of sin, the Lord requires that he come unto Him, mourn over his sins, forsake the sins, be teachable, forgive others, and confess. Again, in the fifty-

57

eighth section of the Doctrine and Covenants, verse 43, we read, "By this ye may know if a man repenteth of his sins—behold, he will confess them and forsake them."

We must always be truly sincere. In *The Adventures of Huckleberry Finn,* by Mark Twain, Huck says: "It made me shiver. And I about made up my mind to pray and see if I couldn't try to quit being the kind of boy I was and be better. So I kneeled down. But the words wouldn't come. Why wouldn't they? It weren't no use to try and hide it from Him. . . . I knowed very well why they wouldn't come. It was because my heart warn't right; it was because I weren't square: it was because I was playing double. I was letting on to give up sin, but away inside of me I was holding on to the biggest one of all. I was trying to make my mouth say I would do the right thing and the clean thing. But deep down in me, I knowed it was a lie, and He knowed it. YOU CAN'T PRAY A LIE . . . I found that out." (New York: Platt & Munk, 1960, pp. 445–46.)

Huck Finn was right. You can't pray a lie; and regardless of what may be decided by a common judge, actual forgiveness cannot take place until true repentance has preceded it. The common judge serves as the Lord's agent. A bishop may be deceived, but the Holy Ghost cannot. When confession takes place, it ought to be from the innermost depths of the heart and soul.

What a tragedy when someone finally gets enough courage to go to the bishop and then leaves his office having only partially confessed. Remember, "the shepherd should not recoil from the diseased sheep." (Victor Hugo, *Les Miserables,* New York: Random House, n.d., p. 32.) The bishops in this kingdom have been endowed with wisdom, judgment, and mercy from on high. They can relieve the burden of the repentant sufferer.

Some years ago, a man knocked on my office door late at night and said, "President, may I speak to you? Are we all alone?" I assured him no one else was in the office. We sat across the corner of the desk, and he said, "Four times I have driven over to the stake office and have seen your light on, and four times I have driven back home without coming in. But," he continued, "last night I was reading in *The Miracle of Forgiveness* again, and I realized that every major transgression must be confessed. I have come to confess a transgression. I have been on two high councils and have served as a bishop twice, and I believe the Lord called me."

I agreed, "I'm sure he called you."

He said, "Forty-two years ago, before my wife and I were married, we committed fornication once, the week prior to our going to the temple. We did not lie to the bishop, who was my wife's father; he simply talked with us and signed our recommends. We then went to the stake president, and he did not interview us. He signed our recommends, and we went to the temple unworthily. While we were on our honeymoon," he continued, "we decided to make it up to the Lord. We decided we would pay more than our share of tithing and more than our share of building fund; we would accept every assignment to the welfare farm and do all else we were asked to do. We decided we were not worthy to go to the temple, and we did not go for a year. It has been forty-two years since the transgression, and we have lived as near Christlike lives as we know how. I believe we have been forgiven, but I know that confession is necessary."

Then he quoted from 2 Nephi 9:41, which states, "Behold, the way for man is narrow, but it lieth in a straight course before him, and the keeper of the gate is the Holy One of Israel; and he employeth no servant there; and there is none other way save it be by the gate; for he cannot be deceived, for the Lord God is his name."

Then he said, "I would rather confess to you now. I am not a young man, and I do not have a lot of years left. I want to be able to meet my Savior with nothing left undone."

I listened to his confession. I wept with him, and when he finished the confession, I told him on behalf of the Church that he was forgiven. He need not discuss it, think about it, or be concerned about it anymore. I told him never to mention it to me again, for I would not remember it and had no desire to. To this day, I cannot remember who it was, although I do remember the case.

We got up and walked to the door together. I said, "Where is your wife?"

He said, "She is in the car."

I asked, "Is she coming in?"

He replied, "No, she can't even think about it except it almost destroys her."

I said, "You tell your wife that I would like to visit with her now. Tell her I want to take this off her heart and close it. Tell her I know what it was that was done, and I will close it, and it need not be opened again. Tell her I will make it as easy as possible for her."

He said, "I'll tell her, but I don't think she will come in."

I answered, "You tell her that if I have to sit here all night, I will not go home until she comes in. I can't bear the thought of her carrying this on her heart one more day in this life; forty-two years is long enough."

He said, "Well, I'll tell her, but I don't think she'll come in."

He left and was gone fifteen minutes, thirty minutes, and forty-five minutes. I was tempted to check the parking lot to see if they had gone home. I resisted; then I heard a timid knock at the door. I went to the door, and there was the sweet woman standing there. Her eyes were wet from crying. She had probably told her husband she couldn't come in. He insisted, telling her I would stay there all night. Finally, forty-five minutes later, she was at the door. I took her by both hands and led her across the room. I sat across the corner of the desk, and then I said, "Your husband confessed to a transgression that happened over forty-two years ago of which you were a part. I want to make it easy for you. I know what the transgression is. Every major transgression must be confessed. You tell me, and I will take it off your heart."

It was like pulling wild horses to get a confession. Finally, about fifteen minutes later, she confessed. I wept; she wept. I told her that it was closed and that I wouldn't remember it and for her to forget it and close it. Then I stood up and put my arm through hers, and we walked down the long hallway to the parking lot. When we got just about to the door, I said, "How do you feel?"

She stopped, looked up at me, and, with tears in her eyes, said, "President, I feel clean for the first time in forty-two years."

A little publication put out by the Church states, "When one has washed his robes in the blood of the Lamb, they are no longer soiled." (Spencer W. Kimball, *A Letter to a Friend,* pamphlet, p. 23.)

One day a woman came to my business office. She leaned across the desk and said, "President, I have carried a transgression on my heart for thirty-four years that I cannot carry one more step in this life. I know how tender-hearted you are, and I wouldn't add one particle of a burden to your soul."

I said, "My dear sister, before you go on, let me share with you a principle of the gospel. When you take a burden off your soul, it is lifted from the priesthood leader's soul also."

She said, "I know I will be cast out; I know I will be excommunicated, but does it have to be forever? Thirty-four years ago, before my first husband and I were married, I was involved in an abortion. Since that time, I have felt like a murderess. It was my husband's idea, and I did not resist. I had an abortion. Later we got married. He was unfaithful constantly during the first two years of our marriage. I finally divorced him and have since remarried a wonderful man who is a convert to the Church. He knows everything; and he still wants to be sealed to me. President, do you think that either in time or in eternity we can be sealed together? I know I will have to be cast out, but does it have to be forever?" The tears flowed down her cheeks.

I had known this woman and thought she was one of the most Christlike women I had ever met. She always baked bread, rolls, or cookies for the people in the neighborhood. Whenever they had a ward party and the Relief Society sisters cleaned up, she always scrubbed the floor. She said that she didn't feel worthy to stand by them and do the dishes after what she had done; she only felt worthy to scrub the floor where they walked. She told me that she had never gossiped about anyone else. "How could I," she said, "after what I had done?"

I listened to her confession, humbled to tears, and told her, "I have never had a case of abortion before. I will need to write to President Kimball, President of the Quorum of the Twelve, and get his counsel."

I wrote to President Kimball and shared the entire story. I told him that she was one of the most Christlike women I had known and that she was willing to submit to any decision he would have for her. Two weeks later I received his response. I called the sister and asked her to meet me at the stake office as soon as she could. When I arrived at the stake center, she was already there. Her eyes were red, and she was pale. I know she must have been on her knees several times after my call, asking for mercy.

Again I sat across the desk from her and said, "I do not want to keep you waiting one second longer. We are not even going to stop for prayer. Let me read you President Kimball's letter: 'Dear President Featherstone: You inquired about a woman who had been involved in an abortion thirty-four years ago. From the way you describe her, it sounds like she has long since repented. You may tell her on behalf of the Church she is forgiven. After a thorough and searching interview, you may issue this sweet sister a temple recommend so she can go to the temple and be sealed to her present husband.' "

If the Savior had been sitting where the woman sat, I would not have felt any closer to him. I believe that is exactly what he would have done. It was as though a two-thousand-pound burden had been lifted from the heart of this good woman. She wept great tears of relief and joy. To this day, I do not remember who the woman was.

President J. Reuben Clark, Jr., said, "I feel that [the Savior] will give that punishment which is the very least that our transgression will justify. . . . I believe that when it comes to making the rewards for our good conduct, he will give us the maximum that is possible to give." (*"As Ye Sow . . . ,"* Brigham Young University Speeches of the Year, Provo, 3 May 1955, p. 7.) I, too, believe this with all my heart and soul.

In Exodus 32, Moses had gone up to the mountain. The children of Israel had fashioned a golden calf with a graving tool. The people offered burnt offerings, and they sat down to eat, drink, and play; and there was great wickedness when Moses came down out of the mountain. He cast the tablets out of his hands, and they were broken; he burned the golden calf and caused the idolaters to be slain.

Then, when the people had repented (and that is the key), Moses went back before the Lord and prayed, "Yet now, if thou wilt forgive their sin—; and if not, blot me, I pray thee, out of thy book which thou hast written." (Ex. 32:32.)

At the close of my interviews with great numbers of people who have confessed transgressions, when they have truly repented, I have felt like Moses who declared, "Yet now, if thou wilt forgive their sins—; and if not, blot me, I pray thee, out of thy book which thou hast written."

Though their sins be as scarlet, they may become white as the driven snow (see Isa. 1:18), and the Lord has promised he would remember their sins no more (see D&C 58:42).

The Lord has provided every soul with a Christlike ecclesiastical leader who has been endowed with powers and keys from on high to be His agent in exercising forgiveness on behalf of the Church. I plead with you: if you have a major transgression on your heart that has not been confessed, go to your bishop. He will be filled with love and charity and will bless your life and take the burden of sin from your heart as a repentant soul in modern Israel.

THE LORD
OFFERS EVERYONE
A WAY BACK

BISHOP ROBERT D. HALES

I received a letter written by a young lady who went on a long, dark journey, a journey that ultimately led her into moral transgression. Her story is important because she is going through the anguish of full repentance and now is beginning to feel the joy that honest repentance can bring. She has asked that her personal experience be shared in the hope that there might be one who can be helped and not take that same journey. She writes (excerpts from a letter):

"It began when I left my home to go to college. Until that time, under the righteous guardianship of my parents, I had not indulged in the loose morals of my friends and acquaintances. Probably the first dent in the armor of faith that my parents had built up around me was the realization that some 'good returned missionaries' were not always so good and really did indulge in necking and petting episodes. I began to think that a certain amount of physical relations were natural and included them in the closer relationships I had with young men.

"Satan is insidious. He leads a person away from the righteous way of living and little by little tempts them into greater and greater wrongs. The months passed, and I fell further and further from the truth. I moved in with a friend who was inactive in the Church and who also had loose morals and drank and smoked. With her I visited bars and nightclubs I never would have gone into on my own initiative.

"Next, I stopped attending Church meetings and even stopped praying. I found that my whole life had changed. I was always depressed. My grades dropped to an all-time low. I couldn't get along with my roommate. Everything, *everything, was wrong.* I found myself totally rejecting the Church and all its teachings. I knew in the depths of my soul that I was afraid. I was truly a 'ship without a rudder.' I found myself searching everywhere for some semblance of security and stability. My parents were physically a long way away. But even at long distance they sensed some of my inner conflict and were worried.

"I finally met a young man, also inactive, with whom I thought I was in love. By then it was easy for me to convince myself that making love was all right as long as I truly felt that I loved the man. So I made love and desecrated the temple of my body. I became pregnant. When I realized my condition, I went to the young man and told him of my problem. He wanted nothing to do with me or my baby. He did say he would pay for an abortion, however, if I so desired.

"At first I rejected the very idea of abortion, but as I thought about it, I began to rationalize. It took me a couple of weeks to talk myself into making an appointment and having the abortion done.

"Shortly thereafter I had the good fortune to meet and marry a young man of extremely high caliber. He was not

67

active in the Church but was and is morally a fine, honest, upstanding man. Ever since that time, I have been working and living toward the goal of becoming active in the Church and of once again attaining a position of righteousness in our Heavenly Father's kingdom.

"A few months ago I realized I must go to the bishop of my ward and confess the terrible things I had done. I did so, knowing that my sins were grievous before the Lord, that I faced possible disfellowshipment or even excommunication. I also knew that the time had come to put myself and my life into the Lord's hands, that I might be able to cleanse my sins and stand spotless before Him on the judgment day.

"I made an appointment one Sunday afternoon with the bishop. He took time out of his busy schedule to hear of my terrible transgressions. Oh, how I prayed to my Heavenly Father before my interview. The bishop was kindly. He asked that I would have the courage to tell him everything, that I would not hold anything back. As I tried to touch lightly on my transgressions and go on, I *couldn't!* A horrible tightening in my throat and chest made it impossible for me to go on. I suddenly knew it was the answer to my prayers. The Spirit of our Father in heaven was with me demanding complete confession. I bear witness that I felt the Spirit constraining me to tell the whole truth!

"It isn't easy to admit past sins even to ourselves. I found that it was as hard for me to admit the exact nature of my sins to myself as it was to admit them to the bishop. I didn't want to think about them.

"After my confession the bishop commended me on taking the first step toward returning to my Heavenly Father and outlined additional steps to prepare me for the day when I would realize that I had truly been forgiven. He emphasized that he, himself, could not forgive me. That was the Lord's decision. He helped me to understand that I *could* be forgiven, that I could gain an awareness of my future goals and not constantly condemn myself all of my life, thus halting my eternal progression. He asked me to read *The Miracle of Forgiveness* by President Spencer W. Kimball. It helped a great deal in making me aware of the process of forgiveness. We had several appointments, the bishop and I, so that he could help me to see my course toward reestablishing myself in good standing in the Church.

"Following my interview with the bishop, I found myself alternating between depression in which I wondered if I would ever be forgiven and becoming lax in doing the things I should be doing. I have learned that to change isn't easy. It takes time. One must learn to 'try and try again.'

"Now I find myself growing ever closer to the Lord — more positive. I know if I continue to work and to grow, *my Father in heaven will forgive me,* but most importantly, *I will also forgive myself.* The important thing is that I must persevere in doing what I know to be right.

"If my experiences sound familiar, I beg you from the depth of my heart to *please* pause and take stock of your life. Do not be misled by the superficial moral codes of our day. They are Satan's most persuasive tools. They have no eternal significance. It is Satan who will *entice us away from* the joyous richness awaiting us in the *eternal family circle.*

"You are sons and daughters of our Heavenly Father. Stay true to your birthright. Do not bring into your lives the miseries and anguish of soul that I brought into mine. Refrain from doing things that will make you *eternally sorry*. Prepare yourselves in righteousness to do the things in life that will make you eternally happy."

This true story is a testimony by a young lady who is coming back from the depths of depression to make a new life for herself. There is no canyon deep enough, no cavern dark enough, to hide from ourselves if we take the long, dark journey. The gospel can protect us from taking the long, dark journey and through the gospel principle of repentance can restore us *even* if we are *now* at the dark journey's bitter end.

The steps of repentance have been clearly defined in the scriptures:

1. Recognize we have done wrong.

2. Covenant with the Lord that we will never repeat the sin we have committed and are repenting of. "By this ye may know if a man repenteth of his sins—behold, he will confess them and forsake them." (D&C 58:43.)

3. Recommit ourselves to living a better life in all phases of the gospel.

4. Make restitution for the wrongs we have committed by (a) repenting in prayer to the Lord; (b) confessing to our bishop, an ordained common judge in Israel and the presiding high priest in our ward; (c) apologizing to those we have offended; and (d) doing what one can to compensate an injured party for the wrong. This last kind of restitution has great meaning where the transgressor should repay for property that has been taken or for debts owed.

5. The depth of our repentance must be as deep as the

sin we have committed. There is no easy way. It hurts, but it also cleanses.

6. Time is the next element of repentance and restitution: (a) Time to prove to ourselves, to our Lord, to our fellowmen that we have committed ourselves to a new way of life and (b) time to study the scriptures and dedicate our lives to the commandments we learn we must live to be happy and have joy.

7. Complete forgiveness of ourselves and forgiveness without any feelings of retribution toward those who have offended us.

8. Finally, the greatest of all blessings: the forgiveness of the Lord. We no longer look back with depression and hurt but forward to the future with hope and joy and love for God, self, and all mankind. "Behold, he who has repented of his sins, the same is forgiven, and I, the Lord, remember them no more." (D&C 58:42.)

"But learn that he who doeth the works of righteousness shall receive his reward, even peace in this world, and eternal life in the world to come." (D&C 59:23.)

I know that God and Jesus Christ, our Redeemer, love us and have given us the gospel to protect us from taking the long, dark journeys in our life. Whether you be a member or a nonmember, the gospel principle of repentance has the power to bring us back from the depths of despair, to give us peace in this world and eternal life in the world to come, even though our journeys may have been long and dark. These principles can apply to all of us — to nonmembers who experience the remission of sins through repentance and baptism, as well as members who repent of their sins. May the Lord's blessings be with all those who are reaching out to know that they may come back.

71

LET MERCY TEMPER JUSTICE

ELDER THEODORE M. BURTON

Many people, both Church members and nonmembers, wonder what General Authorities do. They ask me: "How do you spend your time? I know you travel a lot, hold stake conferences, and speak on Sundays, but what do you do with the rest of your time—just study and prepare your sermons?" When someone asks me that question, I feel like answering, "What extra time?" I prepared this article on planes and in airports waiting for planes to leave. If it reads a little bumpy, I hope you'll understand.

I was called to be a General Authority twenty-nine years ago and had no idea at first what I would be asked to do. I was assigned to hold a stake conference the very next weekend and went for advice to my former stake president, Elder Harold B. Lee, who was then a member of the Council of the Twelve Apostles. I asked him to tell me what to do. His answer both shocked and frightened me. He said, "Theodore, you are a General Authority now. No one tells a General Authority how to act in his special calling. If you have questions, ask the Lord and He will instruct you." I had prayed before, never expecting a direct answer, but now I prayed soberly and with real intent.

72

The Lord did answer my prayers—not in ways I expected, but by speaking things into my mind. But that only happened after I had studied the problem and prepared myself to receive an answer. I have been startled by some of the things that have come to me. Scriptures I had not understood before suddenly were made meaningful. Answers I had previously passed over in reading the scriptures took on new significance. I have truly learned over these years line upon line and precept on precept. I have learned to follow living prophets as well as those prophets who have passed on. Of necessity I have learned to live by faith.

During the course of my service, I have been given many different assignments. Each General Authority is given one or more special duties to perform that occupy his full time. Some are research or teaching assignments; some are difficult administrative responsibilities. Some are highly spiritual experiences such as managing temples where work begins early in the morning and continues until late in the evening. All General Authority assignments require managerial ability, and General Authorities have to bring spiritual and organizational skills into financial, personnel, or other administrative work. The work is demanding of time and energy, and I often marvel at how well my associates carry out these assignments.

One of my assignments was serving on a special committee to assist the First Presidency in bringing back into full Christian fellowship those individuals who have strayed from the fold and who now have reached a point in their lives where they feel a need to regain their full priesthood and temple blessings. Each case requires the personal approval of the First Presidency. Our committee assignment was to organize each of these cases with full information in concise form so that the First Presidency could make a final disposition of each case, based on justice and mercy.

I was sometimes asked the question, "Isn't it depressing to have to review the sins and transgressions of people involved in such difficulties?" It would have been if I had looked for sins and transgressions. But I worked with people who were repenting. These were sons and daughters of God who had made mistakes—some of them very serious. But they were *not* sinners. They *had been* sinners in the past but had learned through bitter experience the heartbreak that results from disobedience to God's laws. *Now* they had become sinners no longer. They were God's repentant children who wanted to come back to Him and were striving to do so. They had made their mistakes and had paid for them. Now they sought understanding, love, and acceptance.

I often wish that in the first place they had believed the words of the prophet Alma that he spoke to his wayward son, Corianton: "And now behold, my son, do not risk one more offense against your God upon those points of doctrine, which ye have hitherto risked to commit sin. Do not suppose, because it has been spoken concerning restoration, that ye shall be restored from sin to happiness. Behold, I say unto you, wickedness *never* was happiness." (Alma 41:9–10; italics added.)

Just as a sewing pattern determines the dress or clothes we wear, so our present lives determine our future existence. Why do people have to go through the "school of hard knocks" to learn this truth? The scriptures and instructions from our spiritual leaders teach us how to avoid the heartache that *always* results from sin.

I have had people tell or write me how much they have learned as they have overcome their sins and thus have brought new happiness to themselves and their families. But how much better had it been if husbands and wives had learned to be kind and considerate, loving and thoughtful, virtuous and true, and had avoided that heartbreak right from the beginning? Many people have done so and have been happy. Others have had to learn to do the right things the hard way before they found happiness.

But the people I worked with were on the road back. So I rejoiced as I organized and summarized each case for consideration by the First Presidency. If an application from a former transgressor was approved by the Presidency, one of the General Authorities was assigned to interview that person to determine his or her present worthiness and readiness to receive back those priesthood and temple blessings that he or she possessed before excommunication occurred. Thus, when President Benson appointed me, for example, to such a task, I interviewed the applicant to determine that repentance truly had taken place.

Then I took time to teach that person how to avoid a recurrence of the problem. Once a person has transgressed, Satan tries hard to discourage that individual and take away his (or her) hope of ever being completely freed from that sin. I explained that God truly loves him and that through the love and atonement of Jesus Christ even personal sins can and will be forgiven, and completely wiped away, if he will only forsake sin and never give way to that temptation again. As General Authorities, we are spiritual healers trying to help people put their lives—and where possible their families—back in order again so that the person involved, if he or she will continue to live righteously, can eventually return to the very presence of God the Eternal Father.

It saddens me when I hear how some of our members and even sometimes our local leaders treat people who have to be disciplined for transgression. I realize there is a tendency to equate the word *discipline* with the word *punish,* but there is a difference between these words. In English, at least, the word *discipline* has the same root as the word *disciple.* A disciple is a student, to be taught. In dealing with transgressors, we must remember that they desperately *need* to be taught. Ofttimes the transgressor is so belligerent that it is impossible to teach him at the moment.

However, if we can remember that he or she is a child of God, we will never abandon him or her. For a branch president or bishop to advise his people to avoid further contact with transgressors is most unwise and unkind. It is at such moments of rebellion or anger when they most need help. We should continue to make friendly overtures to them, not in a spirit of challenge or criticism, but in a spirit of compassion.

The more I study the Book of Mormon, the more I appreciate the spirit of kindness and love with which that book was written. In speaking of those not yet ready to repent, Jesus told his disciples, "And behold, ye shall meet together oft; and ye shall not forbid any man from coming unto you when ye shall meet together, but suffer them that they may come unto you and forbid them not; but ye shall pray for them, and shall not cast them out; and if it so be that they come unto you oft ye shall pray for them unto the Father, in my name." (3 Ne. 18:22–23.)

Unworthy persons are not to partake of the sacrament that they may not mock that holy ordinance in which we covenant to obey and keep the laws of God. The Savior then continues: "Nevertheless, ye shall not cast him out from among you, but shall minister unto him and shall pray for him unto the Father, in my name." (3 Ne. 18:30.)

I understand that to "minister" means we should teach, befriend, and help that person to understand, repent, and return to God. If that person then repents and is baptized, that is good. But if that person refuses to repent, he or she is not yet ready to be numbered among the members of the church of Christ. The Savior then instructs us how to treat those who have not yet repented: "Nevertheless, ye shall not cast him out of your synagogues, or your places of worship, for unto such shall ye continue to minister; for ye know not but what they will return and repent, and come unto me with full purpose of heart, and I shall heal them; and ye shall be the means of bringing salvation unto them." (3 Ne. 18:32.)

I urge you especially to consider the problems that families of transgressors have to face. When a person has to be disciplined, remember the impact this has on his or her family. That family is already crushed by what has occurred. The family has been betrayed and abused, and individual family members often feel the taint of that transgression upon them even though they may be personally innocent. Do not abandon them in their hour of need. Never will they need friends more than at that moment. Never will they need acceptance, kindness, and understanding more than in those first few months after their betrayal. Do not widen the breach. Do not further condemn the offender in the minds of family members. That will only delay the healing process and make forgiveness more difficult. Put yourself in their place. They need strength and encouragement and often financial or physical aid. A spouse left alone finds it difficult to cope with the many changes that have to be made. I ask you just to *be* there — a pillar of friendship on which they can lean, a comforter and protector of the children within that family.

Thus, as one of the General Authorities, and in fulfilling part of my duty, I plead with you to be kind to these distressed children of God who need you now more than ever. May we heed the advice of our Savior: "A new commandment I give unto you, That ye love one another; as I have loved you, that ye also love one another. By this shall all men know that ye are my disciples, if ye have love one to another." (John 13:34–35.)

HE MEANS ME

ELDER MARION D. HANKS

At a family gathering some time ago, as I observed two of our lovely grown daughters, an incident from the past came to mind that forms the burden of my message. I still think of it with a tendency to tears. Another little girl had joined our family and was of course much loved. Occasionally I had called her older sister "Princess," but I had thought about that and, since the second young lady was equally deserving of the royal treatment, had concluded that it would be well for her to share the title, if it were used at all.

So one day I called to her, "Come on, Princess. Let's go to the store for mother." She seemed not to hear. "Honey," her mother said, "Daddy is calling you."

"Oh," she answered, with a quiet sadness that hurt my heart, "he doesn't mean me."

In memory I can still see the resignation on her innocent child face and hear it in her voice, when she thought that her father didn't mean her.

I am one who believes that God loves and will never cease to love all of his children and that he will not cease to hope for us or reach for us or wait for us. In Isaiah it is written: "And therefore will the Lord wait, that he may be gracious unto you, and therefore will he be exalted, that he may have mercy upon you." (Isa. 30:18.)

And yet over the earth, across the years I have met some of God's choicest children who find it very difficult to believe in their hearts that he really means them. They know that he is the source of comfort and pardon and peace and that they must seek him and open the door for him and accept his love, and yet even in their extremity they find it difficult to believe that his promised blessings are for them. Some have offended God and their own consciences and are earnestly repentant, but they find the way back blocked by their unwillingness to forgive themselves or to believe that God will forgive them, or sometimes by a strange reluctance in some of us to *really* forgive, to *really* forget, and to *really* rejoice.

The plan of the Lord and his promises are clear in the teachings of the scriptures. The heart of that plan, as I understand it, is announced in numerous verses of scripture, of which one of the most moving is this: "For God so loved the world, that he gave his only begotten Son, that whosoever believeth in him should not perish, but have everlasting life. For God sent not his Son into the world to condemn the world; but that the world through him might be saved." (John 3:16–17.)

Christ came to *save us*. His plan was called, by a prophet who understood it very well, a "plan of redemption," a "plan of mercy," a "plan of happiness." (Alma 42:13, 15–16.) The Lord taught the letter-bound Pharisees the parables of the lost sheep, the lost coin, and the prodigal son to impress the worth of all of God's children, to emphasize, as he said, the "joy [that] shall be in heaven over

80

one sinner that *repenteth*." And to teach us the nature of a father who, when his son came to himself and started home, had compassion and ran to meet his boy. (See Luke 15:3–32; italics added.) In this and many others of his teachings, he manifested the intensity of his love and of his expectations of us in our treatment of each other and in our responsibility to him.

Reverently I am reminded of the incident of the woman who, in the home of the Pharisee Simon, washed the feet of the Lord with her tears, dried them with her hair, and anointed them with ointment. (See Luke 7:37–39.) The Savior taught the critical Simon the story of the creditor and the two debtors: "The one owed five hundred pence, and the other fifty. And when they had nothing to pay, he frankly forgave them both. Tell me therefore, which of them will love him most? Simon answered and said, I suppose that he, to whom he forgave most. And he said unto him, Thou hast rightly judged." (Luke 7:41–43.)

Then, speaking of the woman, he said: "Her sins, which are many, are forgiven; for she loved much: but to whom little is forgiven, the same loveth little. And he said unto her, Thy sins are forgiven. . . . Thy faith hath saved thee; go in peace." (Luke 7:47–48, 50.)

There is here, of course, no encouragement or condoning of sin. She had been converted by the Lord and sorely repented, and she would obey his commandments and accept his forgiveness. And there would be rejoicing in heaven and should be on earth.

The story of Alma, the Book of Mormon prophet, is well known. He taught these principles with courage and compassion perhaps never excelled. Himself the son of the great prophet, he and other youthful companions were guilty of serious sins. Through angelic intervention, they were turned to a better way; and Alma, repentant and restored, became a strong leader for the Lord. "Wickedness never was happiness," he declared, and gratefully testified also of the "plan of mercy" that brings forgiveness to the truly penitent. (Alma 42:10, 15.)

As the leader of his people, he was uncompromising in defense of righteousness and warm and compassionate with those who had repented and turned from unrighteousness. With his own children, including one son who had been guilty of serious moral error, he shared the anguish that follows transgression and the unspeakable joy that accompanies repentance and forgiveness: "Yea, I say unto you, my son, that there could be nothing so exquisite and so bitter as were my pains. Yea, and again I say unto you, my son, that on the other hand, there can be nothing so exquisite and sweet as was my joy." (Alma 36:21.)

This man of great integrity and no pretense became the first chief judge of the people and the high priest over the Church. He who had cried out unto the Lord Jesus Christ for mercy, "in the most bitter pain and anguish of soul; . . . did find peace to [his] soul" (Alma 38:8) and thereafter taught the people with such power and love that multitudes of them turned to the Lord, obeyed his commandments, received that "mercy [which] claimeth the penitent." (Alma 42:23.)

The message is consistent through scripture. The noble young prophet-leader Nephi wrote the sweet psalm of contrition and faith that is so encouraging and edifying and can be read in the fourth chapter of the second book of Nephi: "Notwithstanding the great goodness of the Lord, in showing me his great and marvelous works, my heart exclaimeth: O wretched man that I am! Yea, my heart sorroweth because of my flesh; my soul grieveth because of mine iniquities. I am encompassed about, because of the temptations and the sins which do so easily beset me. And when I desire to rejoice, my heart groaneth because of my sins; nevertheless, I know in whom I have trusted." (Vv. 17–19.)

Nephi understood that true remorse is a gift from God, not a curse, but a blessing. True remorse involves sorrow and suffering; but the sorrow is purposeful, constructive, cleansing, the "godly sorrow" that "worketh repentance to salvation," and not the "sorrow of the world." (2 Cor. 7:10.)

Through the prophet Ezekiel, the Lord taught us that he has no "pleasure at all" in the suffering of his children through sin. His joy comes when the sinner "turneth away from all his transgressions," for such an one shall "save his soul." (Ezek. 18:23, 27–28.)

The Apostle Paul was disappointed with certain behavior on the part of the Corinthian Saints, and wrote them a letter chastising them. They repented; and when he learned of it, he wrote them again, saying that he was comforted in their comfort: "I rejoice, not that ye were made sorry, but that ye sorrowed to repentance." (2 Cor. 7:9.)

Alma summed it all up in magnificent instruction given to his wayward son Corianton. He concluded that powerful lesson with these significant words—they could be saving words for some—"And now, my son, I desire that ye should let these things trouble you no more, and only let your sins trouble you, with that trouble which shall bring you down unto repentance." (Alma 42:29.)

Almighty God has promised to forgive, forget, and never mention the sins of which we have truly repented. But he has given us the gift of remorse to help *us* remember them constructively, thankfully, and humbly: "Do not endeavor to excuse yourself in the least point because of your sins, by denying the justice of God; but do you let the justice of God, and his mercy, and his longsuffering have full sway in your heart; and let it bring you down to the dust in humility." (Alma 42:30.)

Corianton was sent to preach the word. As leaders, we deal with the most sacred and sensitive creation of God — his children. We need to consider this as we carry out our duty to keep the Church free from iniquity. "Holocausts," it has been written, "are caused not only by atomic explosion. A holocaust occurs whenever a person is put to shame." (Abraham Joshua Heschel.)

It is good to remember what Joseph Smith wrote a long time ago to the Saints scattered abroad: "Let everyone labor to prepare himself for the vineyard, sparing a little time to comfort the mourners; to bind up the broken-hearted; to reclaim the backslider; to bring back the wanderer; to re-invite into the kingdom such as have been cut off, by encouraging them to lay to while the day lasts, and work righteousness, and, with one heart and one mind, prepare to help redeem Zion, that goodly land of promise, where the willing and obedient shall be blessed. Souls are as precious in the sight of God as they ever were; and the Elders were never called to drive any down to hell, but to persuade and invite all men everywhere to repent, that they may become the heirs of salvation." (*History of the Church*, 2:229.)

My child at first did not understand that my invitation was meant for her. She thought it was for someone else. "He didn't mean me." If any need assurance that God's call to repentance and his invitation to mercy and forgiveness and love is for them, I bear that solemn witness.

TIME IS
ON YOUR SIDE

ELDER LOREN C. DUNN

I knew an athlete some years ago who had tremendous talent. He had almost perfect physical coordination. In fact, he was so good he would not train, yet his talents still exceeded the talents and abilities of those around him. It was demoralizing sometimes for those who had to bring themselves to a peak of physical performance, only to have him exceed them because of his natural abilities.

But I happened to be at the stadium one afternoon a few years later when this athlete, who had progressed rather rapidly in a very promising sports career, had what some might call his moment of truth. He was playing with people who had talents as great as he did, and as the pace of the game picked up, the pressures began to mount. He reached inside himself for that great second effort that he always had, but it became obvious that this time he could not marshal all that he needed. That afternoon marked the beginning of a gradual decline, which finally found him retiring from the game years before he should have retired. His original decision to disregard the rules of preparation had, in the end, cost him many years of performance.

Many times we see people around us who violate the

patterns of living and rules that we have been taught to live by, and they seem to do it without any ill effects. On the surface it would seem that it may not make any difference whether we live these rules or not, because those who violate them appear to suffer no consequences. In all ages, it seems that there have been challenges to those who accept these standards as God-given and that they ultimately will carry their own reward. "We are always in the forge, or on the anvil," said Henry Ward Beecher, "by trials God is shaping us for higher things." (*The International Dictionary of Thoughts*, Chicago: J. G. Ferguson Publishing Company, 1969, p. 730.)

These challenges come from many different directions. For instance, there are those who expound the so-called new morality and say that it matters not if a person participates in free love, nor does the marriage contract mean that husband and wife should be faithful to each other. But those who believe this are wrong, and time, which is running out on them if they don't change, will prove them wrong.

"There are some things which never grow old-fashioned," said President David O. McKay. "The sweetness of a baby is one. The virtue and chastity of manhood is another. Youth is the time to lay the foundation for our homes. I know there are those who tell you that suppression is wrong, but I assure you that self-mastery, not indulgence, is the virtue that contributes to the virility of manhood and to the beauty of womanhood." (*Man May Know for Himself: Teachings of President David O. McKay*, Salt Lake City: Deseret Book Company, 1967, p. 250.)

There are also those who sanction the use of drugs, using such reasoning as the fact that the use of marijuana is so widespread that it should be accepted and even condoned, for, they say, it creates no more problems than does alcohol. Those who use this reasoning fail to point out, however, that alcohol disables millions of people each year and that one-half of the fatal traffic accidents in the United States alone are related to excessive drinking. To recommend the use of marijuana by linking it to alcohol is like approving of a hepatitis epidemic on the basis that it probably won't be any more damaging than tuberculosis.

If you are challenged by others because you believe in the law of chastity, because you believe that drugs are not the answer, because you believe in such God-given axioms as "Thou shalt not steal" and "Thou shalt not lie," or because you have a simple and basic faith in God the Father and in his Son Jesus Christ and in your own eternal worth, just remember that time is on your side. Be patient, and the same people who challenge you, if they do not change, will ultimately prove to you, by their lives, that they don't have the answers—either for you or for themselves.

This is not to say that it will be easy. Sometimes the desire to be accepted by an individual or a group causes a person to do things that he really doesn't want to do; but if you can maintain your integrity, you'll come to understand what Lehi meant when he taught that men are that they might have joy—not fleeting pleasure but real joy.

Beware also of the temptation to violate the laws of God with the thought in mind that one can always repent but not really anticipate any remorse as a result of the wrongdoing. Repentance is a great principle, probably the greatest in the gospel of Jesus Christ; and thank heaven the Lord holds the opportunity of repentance out to all.

Yet perhaps it would do no damage to occasionally dwell on the awful nature of sin rather than relying continually on the redeeming qualities of repentance. When our daughter, whom we love very dearly, was three years old, I was doing some studying at my desk at home one day, and she was in the room playing with a glass of water that was on the desk. As she picked up the large glass with her little fingers, I repeatedly warned her that she must be careful or she would drop the glass, which, of course, she finally did. It shattered as it hit the floor, and splinters went in every direction.

Showing the patience of a wise parent, I immediately spanked her, explaining to her that the spanking was the consequence of her insisting on not listening to me by picking up the glass until it dropped and was broken. She shed some tears and gave me a hug, which she usually did when she knew she was in trouble, and the event was quickly forgotten.

Since she often played in her bare feet, I took her out of the room and made every effort to sweep up all the glass particles. But the thought came to me that perhaps I hadn't gotten all the splinters of glass, and at some future time when she is playing in that room, those little feet might find the splinters that went undetected, and she would have to suffer anew for that which she did.

For a young person to violate the law of chastity or some other commandment and then to later put his or her life in order, such action, I am sure, will mean the forgiveness of an understanding and loving God. Yet as that person progresses in life and reaches a point where he or she enters into a marriage contract, and as they have children of their own, it just might be that a splinter of a previous wrongdoing somewhere on the floor of his or her life might prick the conscience.

This is not to say that the Lord hasn't forgiven them, but as they begin to understand the full meaning, the full significance of that which they once did, they may find it unfortunately difficult to forgive themselves. And perhaps this is ultimately the hardest part of repentance, being able to forgive oneself in light of the seriousness of the transgression. Certainly in this, as in all other things, we need the help of the Lord.

Alma told the truth when he taught his son, Corianton, that "wickedness never was happiness." (Alma 41:10.) The teachings of the church of Jesus Christ are for the purpose of saving all mankind from the remorse of wrongdoing; and time is on the side of those who hold to these principles and is working against those who do otherwise.

CONFESSION:
A REQUIREMENT
FOR FORGIVENESS

ELDER J. RICHARD CLARKE

Several years ago, a young man was caught in a serious act of theft. He was taken to jail. His parents were shocked and embarrassed. They assured him not to worry because they had "influence" in high places and were sure they could get him off. Their bishop, though well-meaning, told the boy that he would do all in his power to see that a good boy like him did not have to pay for his crime. The boy finally exploded: "Can't you see what you are doing to me? I am guilty. If you get me off, you will force me to carry the burden of guilt all the days of my life. Please let me pay for my wrongdoing so that I might eventually be set free from guilt."

Few gifts are more desirable than a clear conscience — a soul at peace with itself. Only the power of our Savior Jesus Christ can heal a troubled soul. But if we want him to heal us, we must follow the procedure he has given to us.

Confession is a necessary requirement for complete forgiveness. It is an indication of true "godly sorrow." It is part of the cleansing process — the starting anew that requires a clean page in the diary of our conscience. Confes-

91

sion should be made to the appropriate person who has been wronged by us and to the Lord also. In addition, the nature of our transgression may be serious enough to require confession to a legal priesthood administrator.

"Not every person nor every holder of the priesthood is authorized to receive the transgressor's sacred confessions of guilt. The Lord has organized an orderly and consistent program. Every member of the Church is answerable to an ecclesiastical authority. [See Mosiah 26:29 and D&C 59:12.] In the ward, it is the bishop; in the branch, a president; in the stake or mission, a president; and in the higher Church echelon of authority, the General Authorities with the First Presidency and the Twelve Apostles at the head." (Spencer W. Kimball, *The Miracle of Forgiveness,* Salt Lake City: Bookcraft, 1969, p. 327.)

Those transgressions requiring confession to a bishop are adultery, fornication, other sexual transgressions and deviances, and sins of a comparable seriousness. President Kimball reminds us that "one must not compromise or equivocate—he must make a clean, full confession." (*Miracle of Forgiveness,* p. 180; see pp. 179-89.)

Remember, it is complete deliverance from the tortures of a guilt-ridden soul that we seek. The Prophet Alma says he wandered "through much tribulation, repenting nigh unto death," feeling he was being consumed by an everlasting burning. (Mosiah 27:28.) Repentance is not easy. "Godly sorrow" brings one to the depth of humility. This is why the gift of forgiveness is so sweet and draws the transgressor so close to the Savior with a special bond of affection.

As a bishop, I felt that the most frightening and yet sanctifying responsibility I had was to be a "common judge" over my ward family. I knew how difficult it must be for one to come and recognize the sacred role I occupied during a sincere confession. I knew that I was committed by covenant to keep confidentially locked in my heart the privileged information being revealed to me. And oh, how I prayed for wisdom that I would be able to discern by the Spirit the proper action to take.

I learned that the kindest judgment would be to allow justice to be fully satisfied by a fair "payment" commensurate with the deed. To require less than the transgression merited would be to leave the debt only partially satisfied and would remove only part of the burden of guilt. Compassion often prompts a bishop to be lenient, but leniency without justice is not kindness.

Full repentance liberates the individual with joy unspeakable. Alma said, "And oh, what joy, and what marvelous light I did behold; yea, my soul was filled with joy as exceeding as was my pain! Yea, I say . . . that there could be nothing so exquisite and so bitter as were my pains. Yea, and again I say . . . that on the other hand, there can be nothing so exquisite and sweet as was my joy." (Alma 36:20–21.)

I have been contacted by Church members who have carried a heavy burden on their hearts for many years, trying to serve and donate generously both time and money to pay for their sins rather than confess them to their bishop. They were not able to substitute good works for confession. As President Kimball has illustrated, we must remove all the bad apples from the barrel and start afresh. (See *Miracle of Forgiveness,* p. 180.)

Let's not try to substitute an easier course or shortcut for the Lord's way. Let's commit ourselves today to call upon the bishop and simply say, "Bishop, I have a problem. I need your help. May I come and see you?" He understands that language. Then he, who has been given special keys and inspiration, may help you to start a new and joy-filled life.

BEGIN NOW TO KEEP THE COMMANDMENTS

ELDER M. RUSSELL BALLARD

Being a member of The Church of Jesus Christ of Latter-day Saints is a very special privilege. Understanding the basic principles of the plan of salvation and the principles of life that we are to live by here upon the earth is a great blessing. Some may need to study the doctrines more diligently so they will know the full significance of the covenants and ordinances of the gospel plan and how it provides for us. It's wonderful to know of God's plan to exalt his children. In mortality, separated from our Heavenly Father, we all walk by faith in the Lord Jesus Christ. We must know his teachings and keep his commandments.

The missionary Amulek had some marvelous instructions on this subject. I quote from the writings of Amulek as recorded in chapter 34 of Alma: "Yea, I would that ye would come forth and harden not your hearts any longer; for behold, now is the time and the day of your salvation; and therefore, if ye will repent and harden not your hearts, immediately shall the great plan of redemption be brought about unto you. For behold, this life is the time for men to prepare to meet God; yea, behold the day of this life is the day for men to perform their labors.

"And now, as I said unto you before, as ye have had so many witnesses, therefore, I beseech of you that ye do not procrastinate the day of your repentance until the end; for after this day of life, which is given us to prepare for eternity, behold, if we do not improve our time while in this life, then cometh the night of darkness wherein there can be no labor performed.

"Ye cannot say, when ye are brought to that awful crisis, that I will repent, that I will return to my God. Nay, ye cannot say this; for that same spirit which doth possess your bodies at the time that ye go out of this life, that same spirit will have power to possess your body in that eternal world." (Vv. 31–34.)

Amulek continues: "For behold, if ye have procrastinated the day of your repentance even until death, behold, ye have become subjected to the spirit of the devil, and he doth seal you his; therefore, the Spirit of the Lord hath withdrawn from you, and hath no place in you, and the devil hath all power over you; and this is the final state of the wicked.

"And this I know, because the Lord hath said he dwelleth not in unholy temples, but in the hearts of the righteous doth he dwell; yea, and he has also said that the righteous shall sit down in his kingdom, to go no more out; but their garments should be made white through the blood of the Lamb." (Vv. 35–36.)

Today, tomorrow, next week is the time for our preparation. In fact, it's a lifelong effort; it does not stop until we are safely dead with our testimony still burning very brightly. We ought to reverence life and cherish every minute of it. It should be so precious to us that we feel compelled to commit ourselves to making each day the very best day that we can, preparing ourselves someday to meet our Heavenly Father.

No one knows how long he will be here upon the earth. Therefore, a wise man or a wise woman will constantly evaluate his or her life in light of the teachings of the gospel. We need to look deep into our own hearts and compare what we see in our lives today against what we have been taught about the glorious plan of salvation. Many may find that their lives are out of synchronization with the plan of salvation. If we see something in our lives that is not what it ought to be, then we must have the courage to repent and make the necessary changes immediately.

Think about your own life and how you're doing right now in keeping the commandments of God. Do you see something in your life that is less than what you want it to be? Are you struggling with some habit or behavior that is not in harmony with the plan of salvation? Our Heavenly Father has such great confidence and trust in us that he has given us the freedom to make our own choices in life. Please listen to your conscience; it will help you make proper decisions if you will learn to follow its promptings.

Looking inward into one's own life takes a lot of courage. I know this because I have to look into my own. And sometimes we may see things in our lives that must be changed if we are going to enjoy the blessings of the gospel and prepare ourselves for eternal life. If you know of things in your life that you do not like, ask your Heavenly Father for help and you will find the inner strength to change. Do not deceive yourselves, and never suppose that you can deceive the Holy Ghost. We can deceive ourselves and others, but we cannot deceive the Holy Ghost. He is our spiritual teacher and knows our thoughts and the intents of our hearts.

Please do not attempt to accommodate your habits or behavior by making your own plan or by modifying or adjusting or tampering with God's plan. Sometimes we find people who think that the gospel is too narrow. They think that the plan of salvation is too restrictive and come to believe that God will "understand" if they elect to "do their own thing." Please do not be lulled into that kind of thinking; rather, exercise faith and develop the courage to look inward, comparing your life to our Heavenly Father's plan. The world is full of many voices saying that God's plan of morality, honesty, and integrity is old-fashioned and no longer required. You must never believe anything like this, but rather you need to know the doctrine and live by the teachings of the gospel.

The prophet Alma said: "And now, my brethren, I wish from the inmost part of my heart, yea, with great anxiety even unto pain, that ye would hearken unto my words, and cast off your sins, and not procrastinate the day of your repentance; but that ye would humble yourselves before the Lord, and call on his holy name, and watch and pray continually, that ye may not be tempted above that which ye can bear, and thus be led by the Holy Spirit, becoming humble, meek, submissive, patient, full of love and all long-suffering; having faith on the Lord; having a hope that ye shall receive eternal life; having the love of God always in your hearts, that ye may be lifted up at the last day and enter into his rest.

"And may the Lord grant unto you repentance, that ye may not bring down his wrath upon you, that ye may not be bound down by the chains of hell, that ye may not suffer the second death." (Alma 13:27–30.)

Today, find the courage to repent if necessary. By so doing, you will cleanse your life and you will demonstrate unto your Father in Heaven your love for him. Many people find that making commitments is difficult. However, in my opinion, you will find that you can make some commitments now just as easily as at any other time in your life. Righteous commitments that improve your life now will bring blessings both here in mortality and in the eternities to come.

A few years ago, a friend of mine, a bishop of a university ward at Brigham Young University, came to my office. The purpose of his visit was to seek some counsel from me on how to deal with the moral transgressions his ward members were confessing to him. The bishop shared the fact that in the five months he'd been bishop, seventeen ward members had confessed moral transgressions. He was concerned that more women were involved than men.

This report concerned me, so I looked into the matter further, and I learned that some students have unconfessed transgressions before they go away to college, and other students transgress during their enrollment, but they deliberately wait until they are about to graduate or get married before they clear up their problems with their priesthood leaders. Some of them have indicated that they were afraid to confess earlier because they might face Church discipline that could affect their right to continue as students. I doubt that any repentance deferred for that kind of perceived advantage will ever bring the same cleansing power and peace that a more timely confession would produce.

I now understand more and more why Jesus taught repeatedly that we are to declare nothing unto this generation except repentance. I used to think that was a little narrow. Now I am beginning to see the power in it. As men and women understand the principle of repentance and as they apply the principle to their daily lives, repentance is the process of cleansing, purifying, and sanctifying themselves to prepare them to become Saints. Thus we can all become sanctified, cleansed, and purified through the blood of the Lamb.

My plea is to keep the commandments beginning *right now*. If you have a problem that needs to be confessed to your bishop, then I urge you to see him this week. Don't wait, for he will help you repent and start the cleansing process that you need in your life to remain on the path ultimately leading you to the celestial kingdom. Be grateful that the plan provides for repentance and *be wise enough to use it* when you need to in your lives.

Now we may ask, Why do the prophets teach that today is the day of our salvation? Why do they teach us not to procrastinate our repentance or our other important decisions in life?

My grandfather, Elder Melvin J. Ballard, said: "It is my judgment that any man or woman can do more to conform to the laws of God in one year in this life than they could in ten years when they are dead. The spirit only can repent and change, and then the battle has to go forward with the flesh afterwards. It is much easier to overcome and serve the Lord when both flesh and spirit are combined as one. This is the time when men are more pliable and susceptible. [We will find when we are dead every desire, every feeling will be greatly intensified.] When clay is pliable it is much easier to change than when it gets hard and sets.

"This life is the time to repent. That is why I presume it will take a thousand years . . . to do what it would have taken but three score years and ten to accomplish in this life."

Grandfather continues: "The point I have in mind is that we are sentencing ourselves to long periods of bondage, separating our spirits from our bodies, or we are shortening that period, according to the way in which we overcome and master ourselves." (*Melvin J. Ballard—Crusader for Righteousness,* Salt Lake City: Bookcraft, 1966, pp. 212–13.)

Let us remember that we knew before we were ever born that unless we receive a body of flesh and bone and experience mortality we can never become like our Father in Heaven. He has a body of flesh and bones that has been glorified and exalted. He is our father; we seek to be like him. He has told us we can be like him. He has given us the plan, the central figure of which is his Only Begotten Son, even Jesus Christ.

The Savior is the key to making the plan work in our lives. The more the mysteries of the kingdom of God unfold to us and the more we understand God's plan for us, the more adoration, affection, love, and commitment will fill our hearts for his Beloved Son, Jesus Christ. Our Heavenly Father will bless us with an increase of love for the Lord and a keen desire to serve him, to keep his commandments, and to live true to the plan of redemption and exaltation that is ours.

In section 88 of the Doctrine and Covenants we read: "Now, verily I say unto you, that through the redemption which is made for you is brought to pass the resurrection from the dead. And the spirit and the body are the soul of man. And the resurrection from the dead is the redemption of the soul. And the redemption of the soul is through him that quickeneth all things, in whose bosom it is decreed that the poor and the meek of the earth shall inherit it.

"Therefore, it must needs be sanctified from all unrighteousness, that it may be prepared for the celestial glory; for after it hath filled the measure of its creation, it shall be crowned with glory, even with the presence of God the Father; that bodies who are of the celestial kingdom may possess it forever and ever; for, for this intent was it made and created, and for this intent are they sanctified.

"And they who are not sanctified through the law which I have given unto you, even the law of Christ, must inherit another kingdom, even that of a terrestrial kingdom, or that of a telestial kingdom. For he who is not able to abide the law of the celestial kingdom cannot abide a celestial glory." (Vv. 14–22.)

The plan of salvation is the glorious process by which men and women walk through mortality, with the light of the gospel giving correct spiritual direction. Jesus has shown us the way to live here upon the earth. We can inherit a celestial glory, we can dwell where God and Christ dwell and live with them forever and ever. All of these promises, however, are predicated upon our willingness to love God with all our hearts, to keep his commandments, to repent of our sins, and to love and serve our neighbors and our fellowmen. The first principles and ordinances of the gospel are clear and simple to follow. Through our obedience and willingness to keep the commandments and to serve, love, and honor the Lord, we can purify our lives.

WE LOVE YOU–
PLEASE COME BACK

ELDER RICHARD G. SCOTT

Mindful of my own weakness, yet prayerful that the preparation preceding the message in this essay may qualify me to act as an instrument in the hands of the Lord, I write to bring help to some who are in serious need. I reach out to you who yearn for companionship at almost any price and are tempted to believe it can be purchased or bartered. You may feel excluded from some circles of friendship, but don't look downward for companionship where the price of entry is abandonment of principle and the sacrifice of ideals. The leaders of the Church love you and want your happiness more than you can possibily imagine.

You have learned that fair-weather friends are always available at the bottom of the path that leads to worldliness and unrighteousness and that their companionship always comes with many strings attached. You have seen how each seeks only to satisfy selfish interests. In quiet moments of reflection, you realize that such companionship is hollow and valueless and leads to weakened resolve, compromised ideals, and eventual yielding to serious sin.

To you who have taken this path, I plead, come back.

Come back to the cool, refreshing waters of personal purity. Come back to the warmth and security of your Father in Heaven's love. Come back to the serenity that distills from the decision to live the commandments of your Elder Brother, Jesus the Christ.

You know well the process of repentance and the vital role of a judge in Israel, yet you may have difficulty taking that first step to return. With all the love of my heart, may I offer you a way back. You can begin alone and proceed at your own pace.

I invite you to study carefully the Book of Mormon, to ponder each page and pray for understanding. Strive to apply its teachings in your own life and to find within it the companionship that comes to all who with real intent search its message and diligently strive to apply its teachings in their lives. Through the multitude of the verses that speak of the Savior, the Redeemer, the Prince of Peace, seek prayerfully to know Him. Ask our Father to strengthen your faith in His Son and to plant in your heart a love of His teachings.

May I share with you some of the insight that will come as you carefully study the Book of Mormon. Of his own repentance, Alma declares: "I was . . . in the most bitter pain and anguish of soul; and never, until I did cry out unto the Lord Jesus Christ for mercy, did I receive a remission of my sins. But behold, I did cry unto him and I did find peace to my soul. And now, . . . I have told you this that ye may learn wisdom, . . . that there is no other way or means whereby man can be saved, only in and through Christ." (Alma 38:8–9.) From this scripture you can see that suffering does not bring forgiveness. It comes

105

through faith in Christ and obedience to His teachings, so that His gift of redemption can apply.

You will learn that sincere, repeated prayer, study, and meditation bring a fuller understanding of the atonement of Jesus Christ. Consider His statement from the Book of Mormon: "Behold, I have come unto the world to bring redemption unto the world, to save the world from sin. Therefore, whoso repenteth and cometh unto me as a little child, him will I receive, for of such is the kingdom of God. . . . Therefore repent, and come unto me . . . , and be saved." (3 Ne. 9:21–22.) As you ponder such teachings, your own forgiveness will seem more attainable. As you pray from the depth of humility, with total honesty, our Father will hear you, and the easing of the burden will begin.

By studying the lives recorded in the Book of Mormon, you will see that selfishness is at the root of all sin. It leads to unrighteous acts that bring anguish and misery. You will observe that the antidote for selfishness is love, especially love of the Lord. Love can overpower the undermining effect of selfishness. Love engenders faith in Christ's plan of happiness, provides courage to begin the process of repentance, strengthens the resolve to be obedient to His teachings, and opens the door of service, welcoming in the feelings of self-worth and of being loved and needed.

In time, with the help of a caring, compassionate bishop, you will complete the process of repentance. Then you will have peace and the assurance—even the witness of the Spirit—that the Lord has forgiven you. For some, full relief comes there. Yet there are others who cannot forgive themselves for past transgressions, even knowing the Lord has forgiven them. Somehow they feel compelled to continually condemn themselves and to suffer by frequently recalling the details of past mistakes.

Should there be such a one reading these words, I plead with all my soul that the Lord will touch your heart and cause you to ponder his declaration: "Behold, he who has repented of his sins, the same is forgiven, and I, the Lord, *remember them no more.* By this ye may know if a man repenteth of his sins—behold, he will confess them and forsake them." (D&C 58:42–43; italics added.)

Can't you see that to continue to suffer for sins, when there has been proper repentance and forgiveness of the Lord, is not prompted by the Savior but by the master of deceit, whose goal has always been to bind and enslave the children of our Father in Heaven? Satan would encourage you to continue to relive the details of past mistakes, knowing that such thoughts make progress, growth, and service difficult to attain. It is as though Satan ties strings to the mind and body so that he can manipulate one like a puppet, discouraging personal achievement.

Jesus Christ paid the price and satisfied the demands of justice for all who are obedient to His teachings. Thus, full forgiveness is granted, and the distressing effects of sin need no longer persist in one's life. Indeed, they *cannot persist* if one truly understands the meaning of Christ's atonement.

Ammon, in the Book of Mormon, shows you how to respond when thoughts of past, forgiven transgressions return. Recalling his misssionary experiences among the Lamanites, Ammon said, "Behold, thousands of them do rejoice and have been brought into the fold of God."

Aaron, his brother, cautioned, "Ammon, I fear that thy joy doth carry thee away unto boasting."

Ammon replied: "I do not boast in my own strength, nor in my own wisdom; but behold, . . . my heart is brim with joy, and I will rejoice in my God. . . . Who could have supposed that our God would have been so merciful as to have snatched us from our awful, sinful, and polluted state? Oh then, why did he not consign us to an awful destruction, yea, why did he not let the sword of his justice fall upon us, and doom us to eternal despair? . . . Behold, he did not exercise his justice upon us, but in his great mercy hath brought us . . . the salvation of our souls." (Alma 26:4, 10–11, 17, 19–20.)

That is the secret, stated simply by a servant of God. When memory of prior mistakes encroaches upon your mind, turn your thoughts to Jesus Christ, to the miracle of forgiveness and renewal that comes through Him. Then your suffering will be replaced by joy, gratitude, and thanksgiving for His love.

If you, through poor judgment, were to cover your shoes with mud, would you leave them that way? Of course not. You would cleanse and restore them. Would you then gather the residue of mud and place it in an envelope to show others the mistake you made? No. Neither should you continue to relive forgiven sin. Every time such thoughts come into your mind, turn your heart in gratitude to the Savior, who gave His life that we, through faith in Him and obedience to His teachings, could overcome transgression and conquer its depressing influence in our lives. I promise you that if you will read the Book of Mormon with sincerity of purpose, striving to be obedient to its precepts, you will find two beloved friends.

108

They will change your life and give it meaning and purpose as they have mine.

The first friend is the Book of Mormon itself. It will make you feel good and stimulate you to worthwhile accomplishment. You will be uplifted and receive greater wisdom and insight. That will require much pondering, prayer, and sincere application of the counsel received. In the process, this book will become your beloved friend.

You will also discover the greatest friend of all, Jesus the Christ, our Savior and Redeemer, full of perfect love and boundless compassion, with the power to forgive and forget. It is difficult at times for me to speak of Him, for I love Him so deeply. May the Spirit bear witness of that love and somehow touch your heart that you may find the courage to take those steps that will bring you peace and tranquility, that will restore your feelings of self-worth and place you on the path to happiness.

The Lord loves you; the leaders of His church love you; we need you. Please come back. Don't wait until all is in perfect order. We'll walk beside you. We love you. Please come back.

WHILE THEY ARE WAITING

ELDER MARVIN J. ASHTON

Some time ago a friend, not a member of the Church because of recent discipline, asked, "What can I do while I am waiting? Over the past period of time, it has been made very evident what I cannot do. Tell me and others in my situation what we can do."

As I try to respond to this sincere plea from a good person, perhaps I am directing my suggestions only to a few, but they are a precious few. I would endeavor to instill hope instead of despair in those who temporarily have lost certain powers and privileges. Some of these people in this category dare not hope anymore for fear of being disappointed. May they and their families be helped with thoughts that will bring action, comfort, and a new sense of self-worth.

I recall vividly and with feeling this friend's additional request, "Please don't tell me to be patient, loving, sweet, and understanding. I need more than that. I need solid direction. I have an urgent need to get over my frustrated feelings and get on with my life. Please help me."

How can we as Church members best help these good people? I suggest a quotation from the Book of Mormon

110

as a foundation for our actions: "Nevertheless, ye shall not cast him out from among you, but ye shall minister unto him and shall pray for him unto the Father, in my name; and if it so be that he repenteth and is baptized in my name, then shall ye receive him, and shall minister unto him of my flesh and blood." (3 Nephi 18:30.)

Often in the scriptures, we are reminded that we should minister to all of God's children, that we should do so with the pure love of God in our hearts. George Bernard Shaw once wrote, "The worst sin towards our fellow creatures is not to hate them, but to be indifferent to them." (*The Devil's Disciple,* act 2.) Indifference can be one of the most hurtful ways of behavior. Never should we in life allow ourselves to turn away, walk on the other side of the street, and pretend we didn't see, or prohibit involvement in accepted ways. We need to learn to love everyone, even those who are difficult.

A warm handshake and a friendly smile can be wonderfully healing medicine. Conversely, how unwise we are when we declare, "I'll never speak to him again." Never is a long time, and even those who have caused heartache or shame are not beyond ultimate repentance. Sometimes hurts to the heart are more damaging than physical blows. Yes, they may take longer to heal, but they will heal more quickly if we avoid bitterness and anger and practice forgiveness. As we support the efforts of those who are trying to work through their challenges, we should be helpful, and will be if we can extend kindness, compassion, patience, and love. It is a sad day when any one of us surrenders to sin or circumstances.

Many of those "waiting" have often been hurt by thoughtless words and deeds of those around them.

Blessed is he or she who avoids being offended. There are appropriate and acceptable assignments that can and should be given to those who are in this waiting period.

Now as to the question of my friend, "What shall I do while I'm waiting?" Also from 3 Nephi we are given this warm invitation: "Yea, verily I say unto you, if ye will come unto me ye shall have eternal life. Behold, mine arm of mercy is extended towards you, and whosoever will come, him will I receive and blessed are those who come unto me." (3 Nephi 9:14.)

This scripture indicates that in life there is no waiting period before we can come unto God. In our weakness we know where we can turn for strength. What good advice and wise direction for our lives can be gleaned through study of the scriptures! Self-esteem can be renewed, and strength to do His will can be revived. People must always count more than programs.

As one comes unto Christ, he learns of the reality of forgiveness: "Behold, he who has repented of his sins, the same is forgiven, and I, the Lord, remember them no more. By this ye may know if a man repenteth of his sins — behold, he will confess them and forsake them." (D&C 58:42–43.) When a man is convinced of the truth of that scripture, "I, the Lord, remember them no more," he is ready to start coming back to full fellowship. Some suggestions can be made using two effective words: *shun* and *participate. To shun* means to avoid deliberately and especially consistently, to abhor. *To participate,* one takes part or has a share in common with others.

We would recommend that one should —

1. *Shun feelings of resentment, bitterness, and contention toward individuals rendering decisions.* When discipline is ad-

ministered, there is a tendency on the part of some to become resentful toward the individuals and institutions who have had to make the judgment. We should permit ourselves to take a self-inventory sampling before we "cast the first stone." Resentment and anger are not good for the soul. They are foul things. Bitterness must be replaced with humility. Truly, bitterness injures the one who carries it. It blinds, shrivels, and cankers.

Some of us are inclined to look to the weaknesses and shortcomings of others in order to expand our own comfort zone. A worthy personal support system in cases like this must include, to be effective, family, friends, and acquaintances who are willing to help us cope with what we see and experience. Moroni gave us all some words of advice. "Condemn me not because of mine imperfection, neither my father, because of his imperfection, neither them who have written before him; but rather give thanks unto God that he hath made manifest unto you our imperfections, that ye may learn to be more wise than we have been." (Mormon 9:31.)

A repentant individual will choose his own course and proceed with confidence. He has no need to protect a wounded self. He will not allow himself the danger of self-inflicted sympathy. It is generally good medicine to sympathize with others, but not with yourself.

2. *Shun discouragement.* One of Satan's most powerful tools is discouragement. Whisperings of "you can't do it," "you're no good," "it's too late," "what's the use?" or "things are hopeless" are tools of destruction. Satan would like you to believe that, because you've made one mistake, it's all over. He wants you to quit trying. It is important that discouragement is cast out of the lives of those who

are waiting. This may take a decided amount of work and energy, but it can be accomplished.

3. *Shun escape routes.* There are those who would welcome you into rebellious or apostate groups. We can never build with purpose if we join the ranks of those who criticize and aim to tear down. It is easier to demean and place blame on others for our situation than it is to repent and grow. Some who set out to damage and destroy others end up losing themselves in the process. Drugs, drink, pornographic materials, and subculture associations are also escape routes. Attitudes of "it won't matter now" or "there is nothing for you to do" are totally inappropriate. "Pure religion and undefiled before God and the Father is this, To visit the fatherless and widows in their affliction, and to keep himself unspotted from the world." (James 1:27.) Maintaining and building require discipline and patience. Shun those who would build themselves by destroying others.

4. *Shun the desire to become anonymous.* When difficulties arise, some want to fade into the crowd and become lost and unknown. Any thinking person will realize that there is a wonderful support system available to those who are listed on the records of the Church. There are those who will listen, help, and teach. There will be opportunities to study scriptures, ponder, and pray. Caring people and a caring God want to know where you are. All need to be known, recognized, and loved. Hearts and souls reach out for nurturing and meaningful association. Even those who claim they just want to be left alone are in reality seeking their own identity.

Some privileges and powers are lost when we lose our membership in the Church, but let us not lose ourselves

114

in the process of finding ourselves again. In God's eyes, nobody is a nobody. We should never lose sight of what we may become and who we are.

While waiting, there are many ways to participate:

5. *Participate with your family.* Family members are priceless possessions. They offer love and strength. But even more, family members need each other. You can choose to be aware of the needs of each family member and do your part to help fill those needs. Some need a person to listen; some may need a compliment or positive reinforcement. There is strength and satisfaction in becoming involved in family projects. Encourage family love by being approachable even when you feel you have reason to turn away. The first step back in seeking family acceptance is to change oneself for the better. It is true today, true yesterday, and will be true tomorrow that effective leadership can only be administered through love.

6. *Participate in Church functions and meetings.* Accept opportunities to take appropriate assignments when given the opportunity. I will always be grateful to a man who helped our boys on a continuing basis while it was not possible for him to take part in all the Church programs. He was well loved, and he loved the boys to whom he gave time and guidance.

Practice dependability and commitment. Adapt to existing conditions. There are places to serve where you are needed. When someone declares, "There's nothing for me to do," it just isn't true. We sometimes make that statement because we have learned to live with present situations and resist new opportunities.

7. *Participate in worthy community projects, including compassionate and other volunteer services.* Often our own prob-

115

lems seem to diminish when we become aware of challenges faced by others. When my wife was volunteering as a pink lady at one of our local hospitals, she noticed that some of the doctors would encourage their patients who were depressed, sad, or emotionally ill to join the volunteer organization. That prescription often worked better than medicine to build self-image and restore health to those who found joy in helping others.

As budget cuts plague so many of our cultural and civic programs, there is a place for anyone who desires to work with Scouts, help with reputable drives to collect money, and help in schools, art galleries, welfare agencies, and many other places. There are no restrictions on participating in good works. There are no reasons to wait while God's children are in need of your love and service. Love should be a vehicle allowed to travel without limitations. Jesus was always supremely interested in the individual over the circumstances.

8. *Participate in "reporting in."* Part of your responsibility in coming back is to find someone with whom you can share your concerns, questions, and progress. John Powell, in his book *The Secret of Staying in Love,* tells us that "the genius of communication is the ability to be both totally honest and totally kind at the same time." (Valencia, California: Tabor Publishing, 1974, p. 131.) Look for this kind of person in your life. Problems often seem to diminish when they are vocalized. Another person's point of view may help you gain a different perspective of a situation. It is comforting to have a listener who will share your feelings and respect your needs. Communication should be kind, gentle, open, and constructive.

One of the greatest blessings available to all is personal

prayer. By this means, everyone can "report in" to an understanding Father who loves all His children. God knows the feelings in every human heart. He can soften sorrow and lead when there seems to be no light. Prayer can give guidance and confidence. It reminds us that no one need be alone in this world. If all else fails, remember: God and one other person can be a family.

My plea and invitation to all, especially to those who have temporarily lost certain privileges, is come back. Your lives are as important to us as they should be to you. One of the main goals of the Church is to secure the development and happiness of the individual. We want to have your association and your influence. President David O. McKay once wrote: "In thus emphasizing individual effort, I am not unmindful of the necessity of cooperation. A single, struggling individual may be stalled with his heavy load even as he begins to climb the hill before him. To reach the top unaided is an impossibility. With a little help from fellow travelers he makes the grade and goes on his way in gratitude and rejoicing." (*Pathways to Happiness*, comp. Llewelyn R. McKay, Salt Lake City: Bookcraft, 1957, p. 131.)

We want to be your fellow travelers while you are en route back. Anxiously engage in actions and attitudes that will bring full fellowship and the accompanying joys and rights to which you will be entitled. We will be at your side to help as you travel upward in a support system with God at the helm. We promise you in all the days ahead, that while you are going through what is identified as a waiting period, the quotation from Psalm 142:4 will not be your relationship to us: "I looked on my right hand, and beheld, but there was no man that would know me: refuge failed me; no man cared for my soul."

We love you. We know you, and care for you. We are all God's children, and for members in The Church of Jesus Christ of Latter-day Saints and their treasured associates, there need be no waiting period. Instead we will work together for self-worth and ultimate victory in righteous achievement.

INDEX

Abortion, 62–63, 67
Actions, consequences of, 4–5
Alcohol, 88
Alma, son of Alma, 81–82, 92
Anonymity, shunning, 114–15
Atonement: understanding, 2,
  106–7; reaches the despairing,
  6; start of, 15; result of, 18;
  and repentance, 43, 100; gift
  of, satisfies justice, 54; sins
  erased by, 75. *See also* Jesus
  Christ
Attributes, celestial, 33
Authority, ecclesiastical, 92

Bagehot, Walter, 26–27
Ballard, Melvin J., 100–101
Baptism, 38, 54, 71
Beecher, Henry Ward, 87
Birthright, 69–70
Bitterness, shunning, 112–13
Blessings, 16, 50, 73, 83, 97
Body, healing of, 20–21
Book of Mormon, 54, 76, 105,
  108–9

Challenges, 33, 48
Change: of heart, 3; positive, 5–

7, 14, 17, 40, 46–50, 67–70;
  Hebrew and Greek words for,
  12–13; making a, 53, 97
Chastity, law of, 88–89
Choices, 27
Church of Jesus Christ of Latter-
  day Saints, The: membership
  in, 1–2, 7–8, 77, 95, 114; con-
  version to, 62; rejection of,
  and its teachings, 67; activity
  in, 68, 115; officials of, 59, 63,
  65, 82; teachings of, 90
Clark, J. Reuben, 64
Commandments: related to free-
  dom and happiness, 1–2; obe-
  dience to, 9, 41, 52–54, 57, 95–
  97, 100; transgression of, 51,
  55
Commitment, 14–15, 99
Communication, 49, 116
Community, participation in,
  115–16
Confession, 57–58, 61, 68
Contention, shunning, 112–13
Contriteness, 4–5, 7, 82–83
Corianton, 74, 83–84, 90

David, 48

Debt of sin, 17–18
Discouragement, shunning, 113–14
Drugs, 87–88

Earth, 23–24, 26
Ecology, spiritual, 27
Escape, shunning ways of, 114
Estates, mortal, 25–28, 31, 33–34
Excuse-making, 39
Evil, putting away, 3, 18
Excommunication, 62, 68, 75
Experiences, role of, 29–30, 32, 36

Faith, 2–3, 5, 32, 54, 88
Family, participation in, 115
Fellowship, full, 117
First Presidency, 10, 73–75
Fletcher, Louise, 44
Forgiveness: steps to receive, 15, 37, 58, 71; of self, 18, 80, 90, 106–7; by Church leaders, 20; Lord's, of sin, 20, 57, 71; of others, 49, 53, 55; of God, 89; confession needed for, 91; practicing, 111; reality of, 112. *See also* Repentance
Fornication, 59
Free agency, 43

Galaxy, 23
General Authorities, 72–73, 75–76, 78
God: becoming like, 6–7, 24, 101; returning to, 11–12; commitment to, 15; communication with, 15–16; work and glory of, 18; joy in doing work of, 24; justice of, 27, 84; as Creator and Designer, 28, 32; and perfection, 29; paying our obligations to, 45–46; estrangement from, 51; love of, 52–54, 71, 79, 89, 105; children of, 69, 74, 76, 84, 118. *See also* Jesus Christ
Gomer, 52–54
Gospel, 1–2, 7, 31, 71, 88, 97
Governance, self, 28–29
Greek, *metaneoeo* in, 12–13
Greek Empire, 46
Growth, 32–33
Guilt, 39, 51

Happiness, 21, 25, 37, 74. *See also* Wickedness
Healing, example of, 20–21
Heart: change of, 3; broken, 4–5, 7; hardened, 95
Hebrew, *shube* in, 11–12
Heschel, Abraham Joshua, 84
Holy Ghost, 7, 58, 97–98. *See also* Spirit
Hope, 7, 110; lack of, 44
Hosea, 52–54
Hugo, Victor, 58
Humility, 5, 31–32

Idolatry, 64
Immorality, 4, 52
Imperfection, 113
Indifference, 111
Israel, House of, 53–54, 64

Jacob, 34
Jeremiah, 44–45
Jesus Christ: as author of salvation, 3, 80, 105; suffered for us, 5; has sufficient grace for all, 5; strength of, 6; repayment of, satisfies justice, 17; mercy of, 17–18, 105; transferral of debt to, 17–18; service

as compensation to, 18, 20; as creator, 26; submission to, 30, 98; as men and women of, 34; estrangement from, 51; being like, 59, 63, 65; love of, 71, 75, 109; Spirit of, 96; faith in, 98; our love for, 101; is greatest friend, 109. *See also* Atonement; God

Joseph in Egypt, 49–50

Justice, 93

Kimball, Spencer W., 59, 63, 69, 92–93

Kingdoms, heavenly, 100, 102

Latin in translation, 13–14

Lee, Harold B., 72

Lewis, C. S., 33

Life: present, determines future, 74, 86–87; eternal, 80, 97, 112; cleansing one's, 99; Book of Mormon teachings apply to, 105

Love, 55–56, 102, 106, 109

Marriage, 32, 52, 87, 99

Marijuana, 88

Materialism, 28–29, 52

McKay, David O., 87, 117

Ministering, 77, 111

Morality, 26–27, 67, 69, 82, 87

Mortality, 33

Moses, 64

Muggeridge, Malcolm, 34

Nephi, 82–83

New Testament, 12–14, 54

Obedience, 15–16, 29

Old Testament, 12, 52–54

Packer, Boyd K., 17

Parables, 80–81

Participation, Church and community, 115–16

Peer pressure, 88

Plan of Salvation: of God, 23–25, 54; and gospel, 31, 33; as plan of happiness, 35, 80; understanding principles of, 95, 97–98; process of, 102–3

Powell, John, 116

Power, 27–28

Prayer, 31, 58, 72–73, 116–17

Procrastination, 96, 100

Progression, spiritual, 26

Proving ground, 25–27, 29

Punishment, 16, 27

Purification, process of, 38, 103

Purpose, higher, 37

Rationalization, 15, 47, 67

Remorse, 83

Repentance: as gospel principle, 2, 39, 54, 71, 88; causes change, 3, 39–40, 54; and godly sorrow, 4, 83; process of, 6, 15, 70–71, 105–6; declaring, 9–10; meaning of, 10–11; as matter of great worth, 10; in Old Testament, 11–12; in New Testament, 12–14; and punishment, 14; true, 17, 31; confession precedes, 22; necessity of, 28; and purification, 38; rewards of, 38; as a struggle, 42, 66; as counterpart to free agency, 43; in story of Hosea and Gomer, 52–54; desire for, 53, 63; atoning sacrifice makes, possible, 54; precedes forgiveness, 58; remission of sins through, 71; liberates individual, 93; pro-

crastinating, 96, 98–100; in spirit world, 100–101; helping others in, 110–12, 117–18; things to shun during, 112–15; things to participate in during, 115–17. *See also* Atonement; Forgiveness; Jesus Christ; Sin
Resentment, shunning, 112–13
Restitution, 14, 70
Resurrection, 102
Richards, Stephen L, 42
Righteousness, 28, 48, 50, 71

Sacrament, 54, 77
Salvation, 77, 84, 95, 108. *See also* Plan of Salvation
Satan: deceptions of, 1, 96, 107; and discouragement, 7, 75, 107, 113; temptations of, 66, 69
Self-interest, 104
Selfishness, 106
Self-worth, 110, 118
Service, 18–20, 36, 116
Shaw, George Bernard, 111
Sin: remission of, 38, 71, 105; forsaking, 3, 14, 19, 21–22, 57–58, 70, 75, 102; Lord forgets, 18, 21, 42–43, 55, 57, 64, 71, 84, 107, 112; confession of, precedes repentance, 22, 55; overcoming, 22, 75; jeopardizes Church membership, 43; unrepented, becomes habitual, 51; compensation for, 54,

91. *See also* Forgiveness; Repentance; Transgression.
Smith, Joseph, 84
Solar System, 23
Sorrow, 4, 7, 55, 83, 91
Soul, 20–21, 91, 113
Spirit: gifts of, 4, 7; of man, 4–5, 7, 57, 101; Holy, 43, 54, 68, 109. *See also* Holy Ghost
Support, system of, 113–15

Talents, 30
Time, 34, 71, 90, 93
Transgression: when Lord forgets, 18, 43; serious, 39; feeling unworthy because of, 51, 62; God doesn't condone, 55; confession of, 64, 68, 92, 99; moral, 66; disciplined for, 76; remembrance of, 108. *See also* Sin
Transgressors, 10, 40, 76, 111–13
Trophy, 46
Tupper, Martin F., 48
Twain, Mark, 58

Universe, purpose of, 24
Unrighteousness, 37, 104

Veil, 25–26, 34

Weakness, 5, 51
Wickedness, 2, 12, 16, 37, 64, 74
Worldliness, 37, 51, 104

Young, Brigham, 24